Remaking a Global Cantonese Community with Television and Social Media

Simin Li
University of Victoria

Series in Language and Linguistics
VERNON PRESS

Copyright © 2024 Vernon Press, an imprint of Vernon Art and Science Inc, on behalf of the author.

All rights reserved. No part of this publication may be reproduced, stored in a retrieval system, or transmitted in any form or by any means, electronic, mechanical, photocopying, recording, or otherwise, without the prior permission of Vernon Art and Science Inc.
www.vernonpress.com

In the Americas:
Vernon Press
1000 N West Street, Suite 1200,
Wilmington, Delaware 19801
United States

In the rest of the world:
Vernon Press
C/Sancti Espiritu 17,
Malaga, 29006
Spain

Series in Language and Linguistics

Library of Congress Control Number: 2023949198

ISBN: 979-8-8819-0016-8

Also available: 978-1-64889-049-9 [Hardback]; 978-1-64889-840-2 [PDF, E-Book]

Product and company names mentioned in this work are the trademarks of their respective owners. While every care has been taken in preparing this work, neither the authors nor Vernon Art and Science Inc. may be held responsible for any loss or damage caused or alleged to be caused directly or indirectly by the information contained in it.

Every effort has been made to trace all copyright holders, but if any have been inadvertently overlooked the publisher will be pleased to include any necessary credits in any subsequent reprint or edition.

Cover design by Vernon Press.

To my parents and the younger brother

Table of Contents

List of Figures	vii
List of Tables	ix
Foreword by Nigel Murphy	xi
Preface	xxiii
Introduction	xxv
Chapter 1 **History and Government Policies of Cantonese and Mandarin**	1
Chapter 2 **Dominant Cantonese and Diverse Dialects in Guangdong**	9
Chapter 3 **The Image of Cantonese People and The Censorship Online**	15
Chapter 4 **Civil Practices for Cantonese Prospect**	49
Limitation and Conclusion	67
References	69
Appendix	79
Index	83

List of Figures

Figure 2.1:	The poster of Language Hero Season 4	10
Figure 2.2:	The theme song of the show	11
Figure 2.3:	Episode 1 of Season 2	12
Figure 2.4:	The Episode 1 of Season 4	13
Figure 3.1:	The homepage of the "Cantonese Buk Buk Zaai" on BiliBili	15
Figure 3.2:	The episode "This Canton's Custom Can Help You"	16
Figure 3.3:	The episode "Cantonese Pronunciation Makes You Feel Like Watching Costume Dramas."	18
Figure 3.4:	The episode "Teach You 9 Sounds & 6 Tones in 3 Minutes"	19
Figure 3.5:	The homepage of the Crazy Canton on BiliBili	22
Figure 3.6:	The Episode 1 of the Crazy Canton	23
Figure 3.7:	The example of Cantonese's learning time	23
Figure 3.8:	The episode "No Hong Kong, No Current Cantonese"	26
Figure 3.9:	The homepage of Canton One Two	28
Figure 3.10:	The episode "Studying Outside Guangdong"	37
Figure 3.11:	The episode "It is Time to Prove You are Cantonese for 'Ji Jing Bou Jing.'"	38
Figure 3.12:	The episode "How to Prove You Are Cantonese?"	39
Figure 3.13 :	The episode "the Embarrassing Moment at the Wedding Reception"	40
Figure 3.14:	The episode "When Guangdong Cockroach Meets Guangdong Flying Ant"	41
Figure 3.15:	The episode on Tik Tok	42
Figure 3.16:	The episode "How to Integrate into Guangdong Quickly?"	44
Figure 4.1:	The homepage of Jyut Jyu Baa	49
Figure 4.2:	The themes under the discussion forum	52
Figure 4.3:	The homepage of the Gwong Dung Waa Baa	53

Figure 4.4:	The word cloud of posts' titles	55
Figure 4.5:	The themes under the discussion forum	56
Figure 4.6:	The profile photo of the Cantonese Revival Zone	59
Figure 4.7:	The profile photo of the Gwong Zau Jan	61

List of Tables

Table 0.1:	Eight Chosen Cases about Cantonese People and Cantonese Cultures	xlii
Table 0.2:	The list of the interviewees	xliii
Table 3.1:	The Selected Episodes on BiliBili from 2016-August 2022	17
Table 3.2:	The selected episodes on BiliBili from 2016-September 2017	24
Table 3.3:	The selected episodes on BiliBili from 2017-December 2021	29
Table 4.1:	The Collected Posts from April-June 2022	50
Table 4.2:	The Categories of Posts from April to June 2022	51
Table 4.3:	The Collected Posts from 2019-May 2022	53
Table 4.4:	The Categories of Posts from 2019 to May 2022	54
Table 4.5:	Ten Categories of 155 Posts with Examples	60
Table 4.6:	Nine Categories of 228 Posts with Examples	62

Foreword
by Nigel Murphy

Language is culture. Language is identity. Without a language the culture and identity of a people dies, and Cantonese, the language of Guangdong, and in particular the language of the people of the Pearl River Delta, is no different. The Cantonese language is the heart and soul of the Cantonese people and of Cantonese culture. Throughout China – a vast geographic entity – there have historically been thousands of local languages within the Han populations, as well as the myriad of languages spoken by the ethnic minorities of south and south-western China. Throughout Chinese history the people of each province and county in China spoke their own variations of their local languages. Even adjoining villages often spoke different versions of their local district tongues. For countless centuries this did not pose any difficulties for the people or the rulers of the empire. Ninety percent of the population of China were rural farmers who did not move more than a few miles from their home villages throughout the course of their lives. Officials, however, needed to communicate with each other in order to conduct the business of the empire. A common language that would be understood by officials from all parts of the empire was required, and the obvious choice was the language of the imperial capital and imperial court. With the exception of Nanjing, which is in the south-central region of China, lying on the banks of the Yangzi River, the majority of the rulers of China have resided in the north, and since the Mongolian Yuan dynasty, the capital has mostly been in Beijing. The language that came to be the lingua franca of government was the Beijing and court version of the common language of northern China, now commonly known as Mandarin. The official language of the PRC is a further variation of the language used by the government and the royal court in Beijing, known as Putonghua, or 'the common language.' Historically, however, the language of the imperial court in Beijing played no part in the lives of the vast majority of the 'old hundred names' of the Chinese people. Their local languages remained their sole means of communication and expression of their local culture and identity. For reasons it is not necessary to discuss on this occasion, the languages in the north of China were more homogenous than in the south, mostly being variations of what has now become the common language of China. In South China, however, the linguistic and cultural diversity was a maze of many unique and mutually incomprehensible languages, formed by the histories of the many peoples who resided in that vast region. While the north was demographically static and culturally and linguistically largely uniform, the south was demographically composed of people from a wide variety of regions and ethnic and cultural backgrounds, including from what is referred to as the 'original center' centered in the Yellow River valley centered in the province of Henan. To the people of the 'original center,' they were the only civilized people, all other people beyond the borders of the 'original center' were barbarians, and this attitude has remained largely unchanged until today. Although the people now known as Han Chinese were surrounded by people they considered barbaric, by the time of the first emperor of China, Qin Shi Huang, the population and cultural center had moved from the original northern region to the south, and this trend was increasingly solidified in the coming centuries. For the past two thousand years, the cultural center of China has resided in the south, while the political power has remained in the north, and this has shaped the entire cultural and linguistic history and character of China as an entity. Over time many waves of migration from the north to the south have occurred, following the expansion of Han control in the south. The south of China, was not, however, an empty land. It was populated by hundreds of different ethnicities who had lived in the south for tens of thousands of years. As the northern Chinese migrated south, their encounters with the native people profoundly influenced the migrants both culturally and linguistically, creating new, hybrid, and extremely vital variations of the original northern Chinese cultures. While the northern people clung to their original cultures as a means to assert their claim to be the originators, source, and guardians of genuine Chinese culture, the encounters of the migrants to the south with the native peoples of the south created new and ever-evolving variations on the original Chinese culture. As Li Simin notes, the Kingdom of Chu was the epitome of the new variations on Chinese culture, and its mix of the original northern culture with the many southern native cultures produced a new culture that profoundly influenced and continues to influence Chinese culture. The region that became Guangdong was also under the political and cultural influence of Chu, while Chu was, in return, deeply influenced by the cultures of the people of the Guangdong region. Different forms of Chineseness arose depending on the region where the encounters between the Han Chinese and the local peoples took place, resulting in a myriad of regional subcultures. The main language groups that emerged from these encounters were the Wu languages, which was centered around what is now Shanghai, the Min language group, arising in the Fujian provincial group, and the Yue group, which arose in the Guangdong provincial region. As these new hybrid cultures and languages emerged in the south, the northern Chinese viewed the southern Chinese as little better than the barbarians among whom the migrants had settled. The worst opprobrium, however, was reserved for the Chinese who migrated to the southeastern region of what is now Guangdong, the most southern Chinese province neighboring Vietnam. Guangdong, like its northern neighboring coastal province, Fujian, was isolated from the rest of China by a range of hills and mountains that effectively cut it off from the rest of China, resulting in a distinct culture unique to its region. Because of the mountain ranges that separated Guangdong from the rest of China, the region became known as Lingnam, or the region "south of the ridges." Despite this separation and isolation from the rest of China, Guangdong people – or the Cantonese as they are more commonly known in Western countries – remained, and continue to remain, intensely proud of being Chinese – often considering themselves more Chinese than all other Chinese in China – they were also intensely proud of being Cantonese and of their Cantonese history, culture, and language. Although having taken on significant aspects of the local Bai Yue (Hundred Yue) languages, they maintained the Cantonese language had kept much of the purity of the Chinese spoken in the original cultural foundational region in the north. The successive waves of migrants to Guangdong also took on many of the cultural traits of the Bai Yue people, including their egalitarianism, their independence, their love of freedom, their freedom of thought, as well as their strong affinity to the ocean and their seafaring skills. This led to the emerging Cantonese cultural focus outwards across the oceans for contact with the people of southeast Asia for the purposes of adventure and for trade. While the rest of China looked inward toward the cultural and political center, remaining disdainful and distrustful of the barbarous peoples beyond the borders of the empire, the Cantonese not only welcomed but sought out contact with the peoples beyond the southern borders of their homeland. During the Tang dynasty of 618-907 CE, universally regarded as the first and one of the highest cultural peaks in Chinese history, all things Chinese began to be referred to by the peoples surrounding China as Tang, and this was also applied to the Cantonese and Fujian people who traveled to and from these countries for trade and settlement. One of the earliest references in Chinese to the Cantonese and Fujian peoples who had migrated to southeast Asia was by Zhou Daguan, a native of Wenzhou, Zhejiang, who, in the first year of Emperor Chengzong of the Yuan Dynasty (1296), was ordered to go to Cambodia with a diplomatic mission to Angkor. Zhou Daguan returned to China in July 1297 after staying for about a year and wrote up his notes about his stay into a book. Concerning the Cantonese people he met, Zhou wrote, "The people of the Tang Dynasty were sailors and because they had difficulties in their country, and rice and grain were easy to find, women were easy to get, houses were easy to manage, utensils were easy to obtain, and business was easy, so they often remained there." This is one of the earliest references to the Cantonese as "Tang people." Since that time, the Cantonese, and in particular the Cantonese migrants, have referred to themselves as "Tong yan," their home province as the "Tong Sarn" (Tong mountains), their food as "Tong faan" and later the Chinatowns that grew in the cities of the English-speaking British colonies as "Tong Yan Gai" or "Chinese Peoples'

Street." A further element that significantly contributed to the distinct and unique Cantonese identity was the existence of a separate "Kingdom of the Southern Yue," which emerged at the time of the first emperor Qin Shi Huang, and encompassed the regions of current day Guangdong, Guangxi, and northern Vietnam (Vietnam – Nam Viet -is the Vietnamese language version of Nam Yuet or southern Yue) This kingdom was created by a Chinese official, Zhao Tuo, who was appointed by Qin Shi Huang, to begin the integration of the Lingnam into the newly-created Qin dynasty. Zhao Tuo established his capital at what is now Guangzhou on the mouth of the Pearl River Delta, married a local Yue woman, became assimilated into the local culture, and founded the Kingdom of Nanyue. Nanyue encompassed most of today's Guangdong and Guangxi provinces as well as most of what is now North Vietnam. The majority of Nanyue's residents consisted mainly of the native Yue peoples. The Han Chinese population consisted of descendants of Qin armies sent to conquer the south, as well as girls who worked as army prostitutes, exiled Qin officials, exiled criminals, merchants, adventurers, and others. Concerning the relations between the local Yue and the Han immigrants, Zhao Tuo proactively promoted a policy of assimilating the two cultures into each other. Despite the domination of the Chinese over the Hundred Yue, the amount of assimilation gradually increased over time with both groups influencing the other. The Yi people who lived in the neighboring modern provinces of Guangxi, Guizhou, Yunnan, and southern Sichuan, pledged allegiance to Nanyue, resulting in a broad southern indigenous and Chinese migrant identity opposed to the north, which has continued till today.

As far as the language used in Nanyue is concerned, the Han settlers and government officials spoke Old Chinese and the native Nanyue people spoke Ancient Yue, a now extinct language that some speculate was related to the modern Zhuang language. It is also probable the Yue spoke more than one language. The Old Chinese used in the region was much influenced by Yue (and vice versa) and many Yue loanwords in Cantonese have been identified. Indeed, modern Cantonese is now known as Yue.[1]

The Han dynasty which succeeded Qin (after defeating the southern Chu Kingdom), acknowledged the existence of Nanyue, and Nanyue paid tribute to Han. Soon, however, Han was threatened by the Xiongnu peoples of the north, and, feeling threatened by the possibility of having hostile people in both the north and the south, decided to invade and overthrow Nanyue and incorporate the region into the Han dynasty. Little more than a century after its formation, Nanyue was destroyed, and the region and its people incorporated into the

---

[1] Zhang Rongfang, Huang Miaozhang, *Nan Yue Guo Shi*, 2nd ed.

Han, becoming the renamed Jiaozhou circuit in 111 BC. After the fall of the Han in 220 AD, the Guangdong region became part of a number of regional political entities until China was unified again under the Tang dynasty in 662 AD. While the southern half of the Nanyue broke away during a revolt against the Wu in 262 AD and formed a state fully independent politically and linguistically from China, now known as the Vietnam. The northern half of Nanyue, unlike Vietnam, chose to remain culturally within the Sino-sphere, despite retaining many elements of the Nanyue shared with its southern neighbor. These historical events resulted in the unique linguistic and cultural phenomena colloquially known as Cantonese. As noted, Cantonese language and culture was based on the capital of Guangzhou and the surrounding Pearl River Delta, including the land north of Guangzhou to the border with Guangxi and the eastern half of Guangxi Province. These historical events, the region's geographic isolation, and the unique cultural mix of the Old Chinese and the Yue tribes resulted in a very independent, egalitarian, superstitious, clannish, free thinking, fun loving and innovative culture and people. For two thousand years Guangdong has been viewed by the north as notoriously independent and difficult to govern. The Cantonese saying "The hills are high and the emperor far away" sums up the Cantonese attitude to authority and to orders and edicts issued from the Imperial capital. The Cantonese would obey imperial orders if those orders suited them and ignored them if they didn't. Imperial orders were seen more as suggestions than edicts to be slavishly obeyed. After all, what was the emperor going to do? The mountains were high, and the emperor was, indeed, very far away.

Officials began to view "the south" and Guangdong in particular as a dangerous and barbaric place, with savage, uncivilized residents, and a terrain hostile and even deadly to northerners. Guangdong was seen by officials very much as a hardship assignment and almost equivalent to being sent into exile. Officials who misbehaved or used the emperor or top officials were sent to Guangdong as a punishment.

A famous example of early Cantonese identity and northern Chinese disdain of them comes from the story of Hui Neng, the Sixth Patriarch and founder of Chan Buddhism. Hui Neng was born in 638 in Yunfu, in the west of Guangdong. Although he was born and raised in poverty, after hearing a monk reciting a Buddhist sutra, determined to become a Buddhist monk, and traveled to Hubei to see the Fifth Patriarch Hongren in order to study under him. Because Hui Neng came from Canton and was physically distinctive from the local Northern Chinese, the Hongren told him because he was a "barbarian from the south," he doubted his ability to attain enlightenment. The first chapter of the Platform Sutra describes the introduction of Huineng to Hongren as follows:

The Patriarch asked me, "Who are you and what do you seek?"

I replied, "Your disciple is a commoner from Xinzhou of Lingnan. I have traveled far to pay homage to you and seek nothing other than Buddhahood."

"So, you're from Lingnan, and a barbarian! How can you expect to become a Buddha?" asked the Patriarch.

I replied, "Although people exist as northerners and southerners, in the Buddha-nature there is neither north nor south. A barbarian differs from Your Holiness physically, but what difference is there in our Buddha-nature?

These were not the only differences. Cantonese people's regular contact with the outside world, their eagerness to take up new ideas and innovations from the outside, and their habit of traveling to other nations by sea for trade and migration, as well as the regular visits of people from around the world to Guangzhou, many of whom remained and set up small colonies in Guangzhou, led to the popular Chinese saying, "everything new comes through Guangzhou." As noted, while the northern Chinese have continued to view the Cantonese as irremediably barbarian, yet there are no more Chinese people than the Cantonese. And overseas, especially in the West, Cantonese culture and food has long been seen as Chinese. As Erica Brinkly wrote in Ancient China and the Yue "This book is rooted in a great irony of Chinese history: what was once considered the dreaded ends of the earth during the classical and early imperial periods over time came to represent the epitome of Chinese culture. The ancient Yue, with its associated peoples, cultures, and lands, was transformed in the Chinese South from other to self, foreign to familiar, theirs to ours, and non-Central States to "China."

Victor Mair, professor of Chinese language and literature at the University of Pennsylvania, said national authorities had been promoting Putonghua for around 100 years. "Its primary aim, then as now, has been to attempt to unify the country's language, but it has an underlying secondary agenda, which is the domination of the south -- Cantonese, Shanghainese, Hokkien, etc. -- by the north, Mandarin." Cantonese had been tremendously weakened in Guangdong since the People's Republic was established in 1949, he added. "If it weren't for Hong Kong, Cantonese would soon cease to exist as a significant language."

Cantonese independence has also meant the province was the center of rebellions against northern control. The famous Taiping Revolution, which took place between 1850 and 1864, originated in Guangdong, as did the 1911 revolution that brought the end of the last empire and brought the first democratic Republic of China. The Cantonese have been almost universally viewed by the north as both barbarians and traitors, and the rulers of China have long wanted to tame and neuter the inconvenient and rebellious province, up to and including Communist leaders Mao Zedong and Xi Jinping. But subduing the Cantonese has always been a double-edged sword, as the very independence and rebelliousness of the Cantonese has created one of the richest provinces in China and long introduced new and innovative ideas that have benefited China as a whole. To crush Guangdong is to risk killing the proverbial goose that lays the golden egg. Nonetheless, the CCP has consistently perceived regional identities, regional cultures, and regional languages as serious dangers to Communist rule, and since 1949, its policy regarding regionalism and regional languages has been to promote the use of Mandarin at the expense of regional languages. Its ultimate aim is to create a uniform and homogenous culture and language throughout the whole nation.

This language policy has also been introduced in Hong Kong, universally seen by Beijing as a nest of pirates, traitors, fake foreign devils, white-eyed wolves, and Hong Kong and Cantonese separatists. As with Guangdong, Beijing believes that forcing Mandarin on the overwhelmingly Cantonese-speaking Hong Kong population will help with breaking down Hong Kong's resistance to reintegration into the People's Republic of China. Beijing's increasing pressure on taming Hong Kong has led to a series of protests in the city, the largest taking place between June 2019 and mid-2020, throwing the city into chaos for almost a year.

The paradox of the Cantonese situation is that while the Cantonese have always been extremely proud of their Cantonese culture and identity, they have also been among the most loyal to the concept of Chineseeness in China. It is said there are no more Chinese people than the Cantonese. This has largely been the result of northern Chinese consistently denying that the Cantonese are 'real' Chinese. The issue is not Cantonese loyalty or disloyalty. The real issue is the CPC. It is the combination of the CPC's paranoid insistence on uniformity throughout China as a means of political control, its deep fear of its own people, its fear of separatism, its never-ending need to shore up its own legitimacy, and the traditional perception that the Cantonese are too arrogant and independent for their own good that has led to the determination of the CPC to neuter, to castrate the Cantonese. Their determination to turn the Cantonese into slaves, like most of the rest of the Chinese. Li Simin's book highlights all of these issues. Li quotes an online Cantonese poster stating, "it would be best if Putonghua disappeared from the world...if the northern devils want to exterminate my mother tongue, I will not stand with them in this world...I never view the northern devils as my compatriots." She also notes that the perception of non-Cantonese speakers in Guangdong as being the colonizing behavior of a foreign nation has become increasingly common in Guangdong since 2009. There are two ways of colonizing a land or a people. The first is to physically invade or demographically overwhelm the land by settlers of the invading force. The second is to colonize the minds of the people who have been invaded and marginalized in their own land by forbidding the use of their native language, of expressing their traditions and customs, to denigrate their culture as backward and degenerate, and lastly to impose the colonizers' education system on the children to break the children's link to their traditional language and customs in the future, further exacerbating the death of the colonized people's language, customs, culture, and traditions. This, in effect, is what the PRC is doing in its remote geographic regions. In Guangdong, the means used to impose Mandarin as the major language with the ultimate aim of erasing the use of Cantonese language in the province is to forbid its use in the media, in all official use, and in the school education system. This policy has similarities with the policies of the Revolutionary government in France of the 1790s, which imposed a linguistic genocide on all regional languages with the aim of unifying the country by imposing the Parisian version of the French language. Apart from the policy of communist China, the French Revolutionary policy of forcibly imposing a common language on a nation appears to be the only other occasion when this occurred. The contention of both China and France that a nation cannot be unified and function unless all the people of that nation speak the same language, and imposing a single language is an essential part of nation building is plainly not true. Internationally, monolingual nations are almost unheard of. For example, there are 22 official languages in India, Mexico has 62 official languages, Russia recognizes and supports 50 non-Russian languages. Indonesia has 746 languages in addition to the official Bahasa Indonesia. Nigeria's official language is English, three languages are used in the parliament, and 529 other languages are recognized. Therefore, China is unusual in having and enforcing a single language policy.

If one looks at the example of nature, monocultures are unknown and only exist because of human intervention, and these environments universally become sterile and tend to damage the environment. The same applies to human society. Multiculturalism and hybridity are vital and highly creative, while monocultural and homogenous societies become bland, sterile, and lack innovation and creativity. These dangers have already been exposed during the Mao era, especially during the Cultural Revolution, when society and culture became stultifyingly uniform and homogenous to the detriment of Chinese society and Chinese people. It seems, however, that the CCP is not at all concerned about these dangers, as its language and cultural policies are about political control and maintaining its grip on power, not on maintaining regional cultures and languages. It is clear that nations that allow the use of multiple languages and cultures do not create separatism, disunity, or national disintegration. The CCP has a great fear of separatism, or areas of China that threaten, or appear to threaten, separating from China and establishing themselves as independent political entities. The CCP's fears are unsurprisingly focused on Tibet, Xinjiang, and Inner Mongolia. All three have proved to be constant challenges to the CCP's legitimacy to rule China, and any threats of separation from these three regions have been brutally suppressed. Perhaps not surprisingly, Canton has a long history of threatening separatism and independence. Indeed, between 1917 and 1937, Guangdong was a de facto independent entity. Under the rule of Chen Jiongming and Chen Jitang between 1925 and 1937 Guangdong progressed significantly, free of the burdens and interference of the rest of China and the official Nationalist government in Nanjing. Both were military men. Chen Jitang became governor of Guangdong and between 1929 and 1936 made very significant contributions to the province's development, growth, and modernization. He paved city streets and built high-rise commercial centers, numerous factories and the first modern bridge across the Pearl River. He oversaw the establishment of a public school system with modern elementary and high schools and prestigious colleges and universities (including the Sun Yat-Sen University). People of the province fondly referred to this period as the Golden Age of Guangdong and called Chen the Heavenly King of the South (南天王). This era came to an end with the outbreak of the Second Sino-Japanese War in July 1937 and the occupation of Guangzhou by the Japanese in October 1938. This history of de facto Cantonese independence, combined with the province's long history of rebellion and free-thinking, made the CCP especially watchful of events in the province.

Beijing's language policy has been consistent since it took power in 1949, maintaining the position that the official language of China is a version of Mandarin Chinese based on the Beijing dialect, known as Putonghua, or the common language. This policy was introduced in 1956. Putonghua was made China's sole official language in 1982, and its status as the only official language in China was confirmed by the *Law of the People's Republic of China on the Standard Spoken and Written Chinese Language*, which came into effect on 1 January 2001.

Of course, languages die out from national causes in society, usually when one language becomes more dominant than others. For example, the Seyip (Siyi) language of four counties southwest of Guangzhou has been under threat of extinction even before 1949 due to the rise of standard Guangzhou Cantonese, the prestige version of Cantonese. Languages also die out if they are perceived as rural, crude, backward, unsophisticated, and used by parochial and simple-minded peasants. This trend is exacerbated when the children of the local language speakers are made to use the prestige language at school. In such cases, the children will view the language used by their parents and grandparents as the language of old people and of little to no use to them in making their way in the world. If there is a solid homeland where these languages are used almost exclusively and with pride and as a source of identity, then the language is more likely to survive. The difficulty with Cantonese is that the homelands and strongholds of the language are exactly the places being undermined by state language policy. The state is actively undermining the status and use of Cantonese in the very homelands of Cantonese: Guangdong, Hong Kong, and Macau. For a long time, Hong Kong was seen as the last bastion of Cantonese identity and Cantonese language use. As noted, however, Beijing has increasingly been undermining Cantonese culture, identity, and language as a means to neutralize the potential threat of localism and separatism posed by the city state. The CCP has regularly praised Macau as a model of a successful former foreign colony that has re-integrated with the motherland. Unlike the 'filial and compliant daughter' that Macau is praised as being, Hong Kong is portrayed as the ungrateful, disrespectful, and disobedient older daughter. The CCP still views the obstinate insistence of the Cantonese in using their Cantonese language and cherishing their Cantonese history, heritage, and identity, as counter-revolutionary, rebellious, traitorous, and evidence of foreign-controlled anti-CCP separatism.

The struggle with Beijing over the future of the Cantonese language, culture, and identity, however, is not just about the paranoia and insecurities of the CCP. It is also the continuation of the struggle between the north and the south of China, and the north's two millennia-long disdain for the south, based, no doubt, on more than a little jealousy of the southerners' success and resentment at how the south has taken the mantle of Chineseness from the northern "original center" to the far south and turned what was once the center to the periphery, and what was once the periphery to the center. The long desire to tame, neuter, and bring to heel the insolence and arrogance of the Cantonese. There are therefore two powerful elements from the north that have combined to create a force against the Cantonese and force it into the family of the tamed, biddable, obedient, and unthreatening provinces of China. Unlike in the past, this time the north may succeed in breaking the spirit of the Cantonese. Today, the hills are no longer high, and the emperor is no longer far away. Distance and geography can no longer protect the Cantonese against Beijing.

In July 2010, the Chinese People's Political Consultative Conference (CPPCC) Guangzhou Committee proposed to the mayor of Guangzhou Wan Qingliang that Mandarin programming on Guangzhou Television's main and news channels be significantly increased, pushing out Cantonese. The proposal was criticized in native Cantonese-speaking cities, including Guangzhou and Hong Kong. A mass rally in Guangzhou was held on 25 July 2010 to protest the proposal. Over 10,000 people attended. Similar protests occurred in Hong Kong.

Han Zhipeng, a member of the CPPCC Guangzhou Committee, expressed his opposition after release of the proposal, saying, "Cantonese is the carrier of Lingnan culture, and the mother tongue of Guangdong people; it is also a bond connecting overseas Chinese, for most of them speak only Cantonese."

Guangzhou deputy mayor Ouyang Yongsheng also stated, "Cantonese dialect is Cantonese people's native tongue and is also Lingnan area's dialect. Guangzhou according to law, according to rule, according to heart, according to reason would never do something to 'promote Mandarin while abolishing Cantonese.'" Guangzhou TV rejected the proposal, citing "historic causes and present demands" as reasons for Cantonese-Mandarin bilingualism.

Nonetheless, Beijing has systematically increased the pressure on local and non-standard languages. In 2012 further restrictions were introduced on the use of the Cantonese language with the Guangdong National Language Regulations, which promoted the use of Standard Mandarin Chinese in broadcast and print media at the expense of Cantonese and other related dialects. The new regulation policy was labeled by Cantonese as a "pro-Mandarin, anti-Yue" legislation (废粤推普 or 推普废粤). The following year, in 2013, China's Education Ministry stated that about 400 million people were still unable to speak Mandarin. That year the government pushed linguistic unity in China, focusing on the countryside and areas with ethnic minorities. In September 2020, the CCP announced that from mid-2021 Mandarin would be the only language used as the medium for teaching in schools across the country.

These pressures on non-Putonghua language use in China will continue until Beijing's aim of a single, uniform, national language used by all throughout China has been accomplished. The examples of resistance and the valiant attempts of some Cantonese to preserve their culture, history, language, and identity against the colonization of Guangdong by Beijing, while immensely inspiring, do have the feeling of the mouse standing its ground and spitting in the face of the cat that is about to eat it. It also raises the question of whether these acts of resistance against the forced imposition of Mandarin are merely delaying the inevitable. The reality of the fragility of Cantonese in the face of the seemingly limitless power of the CPC to impose its will on anyone in China fills many, this author included, with great foreboding for the future of the Cantonese in China and internationally. It can only be hoped, for those who wish to see the survival and flourishing and growth of the intangible cultural treasure of the world, that the efforts of the people described by Li Simin in this book, as well as others, will ensure that outcome and ensure the continuing existence of the Cantonese language, history, culture, and identity.

Nigel Murphy
4 November 2023.

Preface

Writing on the relationships between language and identity has proven to be a challenge. I distinctly recall the time when I submitted an incomplete proposal to my then-supervisor, Dr. Guoguang Wu. He seriously quipped that it resembled a declaration of Cantonese independence. Although voices advocating for independence do exist on the internet, academic research on this subject has often felt like a distant dream. Unlike the vigorous research scene in Hong Kong, where the political landscape has undergone rapid transformations since 2014, nationalism in Guangdong is less conspicuous. Consequently, my journey from conceiving the thesis proposal to completing this book has been marked by an ongoing struggle to define its research position within the intricate relationship between language and identity.

Furthermore, the writing process brought unexpected challenges. In the summer of 2019, I had meticulously planned a visit to Guangzhou, reaching out to a professor at Jinan University and another at the Chinese University of Hong Kong to discuss the possibility of a visiting scholar program via emails. My university had also offered funding support for a field trip beyond Canada, where I aimed to gather academic materials on the Cantonese language, conduct interviews with the show producers in Guangzhou, and seek guidance from linguistic scholars. However, the outbreak of Covid-19 and the months long protests in Hong Kong abruptly disrupted my plans. I never imagined that the pursuit of my second master's degree could potentially be life-threatening. Consequently, I had to relinquish my original data collection method and adapt to an online approach.

Additionally, the process of reading and writing was far from smooth. As one of the early English-language researchers in Guangdong Cantonese studies, I grappled with limited reference literature, the reluctance of interviewees to participate online, and the ever-increasing cost of living in Vancouver. Particularly for interviewees within Guangdong, expressing any opinions during the era of Xi Jinping posed significant risks. Hence, I extend my heartfelt gratitude to the five interviewees whose contributions are featured in this book. The responsibility to preserve my mother tongue and honor my hometown consistently motivated me to complete this work despite the moments when thoughts of giving up crossed my mind. In this regard, I am deeply appreciative of my parents' financial support for both my research and my livelihood in Vancouver.

This book has something to offer everyone, regardless of age or background. For those residing in mainland China, it's a journey back in time. Older

Cantonese speakers will reminisce about their childhood, with memories of delicious Cantonese food, playful children's songs, and cherished customs. Even those who aren't native Cantonese speakers will recall the Cantonese TV shows, movies, and music that colored their youth. Younger readers will find familiar elements in the short videos they currently enjoy. For language preservation advocates, this book sheds light on Cantonese speakers' efforts to protect their native language and the challenges they face. For readers outside of mainland China, it offers insights into the country's internal changing landscape, especially grassroots practices and identities. By blending the disciplines of linguistics, political science, and communication, this book provides a broad perspective on how language is intertwined with our sense of belonging.

Simultaneously, my research focus underwent a significant shift. Contrasting with the time I spent writing my first book, "Discourses of Asian societies: cases from China, Hong Kong, and Taiwan," from 2014 to 2019, I transitioned from social dynamics and international relations in the Asia Pacific region to a more localized approach. The inspiration for this shift emerged from my recent observations and research experiences in Taiwan and Hong Kong, leading me to concentrate on Guangdong and its global diaspora. Guided by my research intuition into China's internal dynamics and its external relationships, I formed the belief that overseas studies would assume increasing importance. Consequently, I hold the expectation that the future will see a surge in Guangdong studies and scholars with Guangdong backgrounds.

Lastly, I wish to express my sincere gratitude to my supervisor, Dr. Xu, who spared no effort in supporting my research, as well as Dr. Chau and Dr. Chong, friends from London, Victoria, Vancouver, and the United States, who provided invaluable advice or emotional support. Furthermore, I extend my thanks to the scholars from Canada and New Zealand who contributed the book blub and book foreword. The challenges I encountered during the pandemic were numerous, but I am immensely fortunate to have had these individuals by my side. It is my hope that this book not only offers fresh perspectives on local studies but also serves as an inspiration to emerging scholars.

Simin Li
Vancouver

Introduction

A speech-community is a group of people who interact by means of speech...Chinese as the largest speech-community...but the term Chinese denotes a family of mutually unintelligible languages...Cantonese, probably ranks among the largest speech-community.[1]

Leonard Bloomfield

Language, and particularly a fully developed language, is a fundamental attribute of self-recognition, and of the establishment of an invisible national boundary less arbitrary than territoriality, and less exclusive than ethnicity.[2]

Manuel Castells

The sun never sets on Cantonese society; where there is salt water, there is Hakka people; where there is tide, there is Teochew people.

The prevalent proverb among three subgroups of Guangdong

In the Summer of 2010, a rare and highly visible protest called "Shoring up Cantonese" (Caang Jyut Jyu 撑粤語) occurred in Guangzhou, Guangdong province of China. It was triggered by a proposal that advocated a local TV station to broadcast in Mandarin. The concern about the decline of Cantonese (Jyut Jyu 粤語) was ignited among the residents, and thousands of protesters rallied on 25 July 2010 (Branigan, 2010). However, the protest did not improve the status of Cantonese because, after one year, the provincial government issued the rule, echoing the national language policy, that using Mandarin as the basic language in governments, schools, and media, and only the approved dialects can be broadcasted (BBC, 2011). Consequently, Guangzhouers' concern over Cantonese continues, but the battleground shifts to cyberspace. To protect and promote Cantonese language and Cantonese culture, an array of Cantonese shows produced and spread by the younger Cantonese speakers of Guangdong are burgeoning on various social media in recent years.

The internet, or more explicitly, information and communications technologies help to facilitate political expression, communication, and mobilization. It

---

[1] Bloomfield, L. (1935). Language. New York: HarperCollins.

[2] Castells, M. (2004). The Power of Identity the Information Age Economy, Society and Culture, Volume II. Blackwell Oxford.

provides a public space for citizens to express discontent and criticize officials and policies as well as expose wrongdoings of government and corporations (deLisle, Goldstein, & Yang, 2016). Therefore, the expansion of civil activities and the formation of civil society are expected with the development of technologies. Moreover, personalized expression online challenges publishing norms and creates new culture. By historicizing BBS, the blog, the microblog, and WeChat and investigating how user-generated content has been promoted, debated, censored, and commodified on the Chinese internet, Guo (2020) argues that the age of innocence and idealism has evolved into the age of commerce and pragmatism among the complex interactions of multiple actors including state, cultural institutions, commercial entities, and internet users. Yuan (2021) contends that through the competitions of multiple actors with symbolic practices, these symbolic practices acquire forms, functions, and meanings via the Internet as well as provide contexts for discourses of new social identities and relations. The Internet also changes the cultural politics of the public voice by empowering new network spaces, symbolic resources, forms of sociality, and struggles for power (Yuan, 2021). To those ethnic groups without a nation, Vergani and Zuev (2011) argue that the creation of visual and audio contents on the internet propagates their unifying emotional bases and serves as a means to devise symbolic codes. On the other hand, language is more than an instrument to communicate. It is usually considered to be a primary force to build and unite a national identity (Grzywacz, 2012). According to Anderson (1991, p. 133), language has the capacity to build particular solidarities through the administrative and education system. For example, Portuguese, spoken in Mozambique, is the medium used to imagine Mozambique, similar to how Portuguese is associated with Brazil (Anderson, 1991, p. 134).

Considering the significant number of Cantonese speakers worldwide[3] and the international influence of Cantonese, and inspired by the growing popularity of Cantonese shows online, the book is interested in asking the following questions to explore the potential of a global language community. 1. To what extent does Cantonese assist the creation of a collective identity? 2. How is Cantonese represented on TV and social media? 3. How does the Chinese government's restriction on the internet affect Cantonese representation on social media? 4. How does the content creation inform Cantonese community building and affect the creation of collective identity?

In Mainland China, Cantonese is regarded as a dialect, while Mandarin, also known as "Putonghua," is recognized as the national language and usually

---

[3] Cantonese is spoken in Guangdong, Guangxi, Hong Kong, Macau, and by overseas Chinese, with a population estimated to be around 120 million.

viewed as standard Chinese language (Zhong Wen 中文). However, Cantonese is almost the most influential dialect of China. Its flourishing and decline are closely associated with China's economy. Guangzhou, also known as Canton, derives its name from the Wu dynasty of the Three Kingdoms period (220-280). It has been a well-known port and transportation hub for over a thousand years. Since the Six Dynasties period (265-581), Guangzhou has forged an important trade network with Southeast Asia and, in the Tang dynasty (618-907), it became a major focal point for trade with the Arab empire (Graham, 2002). Its role in trade is particularly indispensable when the country isolates itself. Notably, it was the sole port for foreign traders' access from 1759 to 1842 and during the Mao era (1949-1976). [4] Therefore, as the lingua franca of Guangzhou, Cantonese not only has a long history but also absorbs many English words. Quite a few daily phrases spoken in Cantonese are translated or evolved from English, which makes Cantonese more vivid and inclusive. When China reopened to the world in the 1970s, with a thirst for capital, technologies, and talents, Cantonese was pursued by people from elsewhere within China as it was a link with the special administrative region, Hong Kong and overseas Chinese, whose origins were mainly Cantonese. It was viewed as an advanced, open, and fashionable language as well as the tool to unify the people out of China (Luqiu, 2018). Meanwhile, the entertainment industry of Hong Kong promoted its popularity (He, 2018). Until now, Guangdong province is still the only area within China that can receive Hong Kong's TV programs at home.

Moreover, Guangdong's status during the reopening period strengthens the influence of Cantonese. Benefiting from the reopening policy and the longstanding trade traditions, Guangdong acquired many preferential treatments. Alongside the reception of Cantonese and English TV programs made by two Hong Kong television broadcasting companies, Television Broadcasts Limited (TVB) and Asia Television Limited (ATV) in the 1990s, it also has introduced other non-mainland China's TV channels, such as Xing Kong, ever owned by the News Corp, China Entertainment Television owned by the TOM Group and the Turner Broadcasting System, and the Macau Asia Satellite Television since early 2000s. It needs to be emphasized that all mass media are controlled and managed by the government. The above TV channels were permitted to broadcast in the Guangdong area only by producing their own shows and purchasing movies, dramas, and variety shows from Taiwan, Korea, Japan, and so on. Therefore, the residents of Guangdong had more opportunities to access different cultures and ideas than the residents of other provinces and formed unique memories during their growing experience. To compete with Hong

---

[4] Canton Fair (廣交會) established in 1957 in Guangzhou was the only place to handle trades with nonsocialist countries.

Kong as the first dialect satellite channel within China, Television Southern (TVS) was founded in Guangzhou and started to broadcast to global Cantonese speakers in 2004.

The uniqueness of Cantonese and its popularity among overseas Chinese, on the one hand, made it more prominent in the world. Apart from the existence of physical Cantonese research associations, advocacy organizations, virtual alliances, and databases, an international conference on Cantonese studies has been organized by the scholars of Guangdong, Hong Kong, and Macau since 1987, which is probably the largest and longest-running event dedicated to dialect studies.[5] Within the overseas Chinese community, it is the only dialect that can be on equal footing with Mandarin. For instance, in Vancouver, Canada, knowing Mandarin and Cantonese is a plus in a job posting for a Chinese company or serving Chinese customers. Sometimes, knowing Cantonese is preferable. In many ethnic Chinese eyes, Cantonese is a language, not a dialect.

Nevertheless, the popularity of Mandarin shrinks the space of Cantonese identity construction in Guangdong under the national Mandarin promotion policy. The massive influx of migrant workers and the speedy urbanization and internationalization of China after the mid-2000s also led to Cantonese at risk of dying. The policies of banning Cantonese on campus, social media, or private companies are exposed from time to time and always cause native speakers' strong resistance. The most recent one is the rule of a Sushi restaurant located in Guangzhou that forbade local employees from speaking Cantonese among Mandarin-speaking employees (Guo, 2022). Further, the rise of nationalism and the stagnant Cantonese entertainment industry shape the local younger generation's attitude to Cantonese. More and more news reports and local parents find teenagers and children of Guangdong, especially in the Pearl River Delta area, are not able or willing to speak Cantonese (Lau, 2014; Sonmez, 2014; He, 2018). Hong Kong and Macau, where Cantonese enjoys official status, face a similar situation (Fok & Ma, 2018; Lai, 2021). According to the official survey, the proportion of the population aged 5 and over in Cantonese as usual spoken language drops to 88.2% in 2021 from 89.5% in 2011 in Hong Kong, while the number aged 3 and over in Macau drops to 80.1% in 2016 from 83.4% in 2011 (Census and Statistics Department, 2022; Statistics and Census Service, 2017).

In fact, other dialects, such as Hokkien and Wu language in China, are also declining in varying degrees. However, the disputes on Cantonese are almost

---

[5] The introduction of the international conference of Yue dialects (國際粵方言研討會) can be found at http://www.cuhk.edu.hk/ics/clrc/yue_dialects/index.html

the most evident. On the vibrant online learning and communicating community "Zhihu," Cantonese as a topic has collected over 4500 questions and is followed by more than 40000 users.[6] "How should we view Cantonese being insisted upon by some people in Guangdong" is an example of a much commented on user question. In some people's eyes, speaking Cantonese in Guangzhou is a question, but the discussion was banned shortly after being posted because it "caused confrontation among the users in website."[7]

In contrast to the important roles of Cantonese in culture, economy, and politics, the development of Cantonese cultural products is limited in China. Nearly all well-known Cantonese movies, music, and dramas in the world are made by Hong Kong. The drama "*The King of Naam Jyut*" (Nan Yue Wang 南越王) is a case in point. It was probably the first drama made by a film and TV production company in Guangzhou to introduce the little-known history of the Naam Jyut empire.[8] However, it was banned after completion in 2007, but no official explanation was given. Netizens suggested that reasons for banning might include the extreme topic, the risk of national unification, and the advocacy of independence.[9]

Nonetheless, the advance of communication technologies makes various contents and opinions more accessible. For example, the history of the Naam Jyut empire can be approached on the Internet when traditional media is less available. Given the above, the book argues that Cantonese is able to become a fully developed language, and a global Cantonese community is possible. In conjunction with the wide access to the Internet, Cantonese, as an old language, provides abundant resources for the creation of content on social media. The barely known history and knowledge of Cantonese, which are never taught in mainland China's public education system are demonstrated in the creation of it. Therefore, a unique image of Cantonese people is being built online in the global network. However, factors such as state nationalism, the imbalance between spoken Cantonese and written Cantonese, censorship and self-censorship by administrators, platforms, and creators, and the gaps between Guangdong and other provinces in economic levels, lifestyles and values present obstacles to the development of Cantonese. Cantonese protectors and promoters within China therefore need to find new ways to refresh and

---

[6] The data can be retrieved from https://www.zhihu.com/topic/19557795/intro

[7] The reason can be found at https://www.zhihu.com/question/33630925

[8] Naam Jyut was the first empire in the Ling Nan (嶺南) region seceding from the Central Kingdom and set Guangzhou as its capital for 93 years. Its ruling range included Guangdong, Guangxi, Fujian, and Vietnam.

[9] The discussion can be found at https://movie.douban.com/subject/25851757/

popularize Cantonese language amidst intense competition in cultural production.

On the other hand, the Cantonese speakers in Guangdong realize that they do not have the right or power to determine which language to use. Consequently, doubts and criticisms of government policies, as well as the distinctions between Cantonese and Mandarin speakers, are expressed and confirmed through their content generation. Talking about the formation of Cantonese nation may be too early, but the sense of nation consciousness rooted in the Cantonese language is emerging through the internet.

The remainder of the book is structured as follows. The next section is a literature review, which provides the history of the formation of Chinese nationalism and explores the evolution of civic engagement in Chinese digital media. After that, the book introduces the research methods and eight chosen cases. The book argues that Mandarin promotion campaign curbs dialects, so the first chapter examines the relationship between Cantonese and Mandarin from history and policies. Then, the book analyzes eight cases of content generation and digital practices with visual data from chapter two to chapter four. At last, the book concludes the findings and research limitations.

Literature Review

The review argues that there is a relationship between language and identity. Therefore, in the first section, it is necessary to examine the definition of nationalism from the premodern to the modern era and analyze the case of Chinese nationalism. Indeed, one can argue that Chinese nationalism is a product of modernity. The Chinese state maintains that the national language plays a vital role in unifying the Chinese population. However, globalization and the development of communication technologies give rise to various manifestations and diverse forms of nationalism, which are usually out of state control. The transformative role of the internet in China then makes the review investigate the power of digital media and the related digital practices in the second section. In the heavily regulated internet, the battles between censorship and anti-censorship from the government and netzines are heightened.

General literature on nationalism

Understanding nationalism is crucial to comprehending the analysis disclosed in this book. Starting from its nature, at least three paradigms explain how it emerges: primordialism, perennialism, and modernism (Greenfeld & Eastwood, 2009). From the onset, it is essential to understand that different perspectives exist for conceptualizing nationalism. Van den Berghe (Ozkirimli, 2010, p. 54) claims that in the view of primordialism, a nation is the extension of kinship from smaller kin units, and kinship constructs the basic of nationalism. For the perennialism, Hastings (1997) defines a nation as a self-conscious group of people with a shared cultural identity and spoken language; thus nationalism becomes a brief to defend the nation. As a reaction to the above two paradigms, another approach featuring the era of modernization appears. Gellner (1983) argues that nationalism as a political principle is about the link between state and culture. Nation merely emerges when standardized, homogeneous, and centrally sustained high cultures pervade the whole population (Gellner, 1983, p. 55). In Gellner's opinion, nationalism gives rise to a nation. For further examination of nationalism, Anderson (1991) argues that its definition should extend beyond political and cultural factors and defines a nation as an imagined political community. In his explanation, reading the same printed book or newspaper builds connections among people who have never met in person. Thus, print languages and print technology generate national consciousness (Anderson, 1991, p. 46). Furthermore, Calhoun (2007) extends the definition that nationalism is a discursive formation. By talking, writing, and thinking on the units of culture, politics, and belonging, nation is constructed (Calhoun, 2007, p. 27). In a word, these interpretations are situated in a European context.

However, to the non-European world, especially the post-colonial states, Chatterjee proposes a different modular form of modern community. He argues (1993) that nationalism has a material domain occupied by the West and a spiritual domain preserved by the colonized state. Therefore, what nationalists in the third world should do is to fashion the non-Western national culture to fit the modern world (Chatterjee, 1993, p. 6). At this point, the intellectual elites' role is extremely significant in nation-building of the non-Western world. In the postcolonial states, as Rejai and Enloe (1969, p. 151) note, the indigenous rulers utilize nationalism to maintain and expand the functions of state. They integrate the nation with a shared national language, common religion, and economic development project (Rejai & Enloe, 1969, p. 153-154).

In summary, the above discussion can be categorized into two types of nationalism. One is popular nationalism, in which a group of people with common cultural attributes have the authority to manage affairs by creating an independent state, while the other is state nationalism, in which government or agents within a state have a sense to create a nation (Harris, 1997). The colonial and post-colonial states are usually in the second category.

Chinese nationalism

Generally, scholars use culturalism to define premodern China before nationalism appears (Harrison, 1969; Townsend, 1992). As Zhao (2004, p. 41) explains, culturalism as a cultural identity based on the Confucian cultural system convicts cultural superiority and rejects equality among states. Nation and state, if they exist in the traditional Chinese order, merely serve culture, not a particular nation (Zhao, 2004, p. 41). It is widely accepted that nationalism emerged after China was confronted with conflicts with other empires, especially British and Japan, during the nineteenth and twentieth centuries, and the concept of nation state was introduced by a small group of intellectuals (e.g., Zhao, 2004; Weatherley & Zhang, 2017). Zhao (2004, p. 46) points out that nationalism replaces culturalism as the dominant view by reviewing the historical records of new terms "Minzu" (nation), "Zhonghua minzu" (Chinese nation), and "Hanren" (Han ethnicity). Chang (2001, p. 16) examines the relationship between a nation and a state, highlighting that a nation can secure its material means of livelihood and protect itself from external aggressors through its land and government, while the survival of the state relies on the solidarity feelings of nation. Thus, nationalism, the feeling of love and loyalty to a nation, was used by intellectuals to solve the problems caused by imperialism (Chang, 2001). To some, language is essential to national identity and even equivalent to nation itself (Guo, 2003, p. 92). In the eyes of Chinese nationalists, China was defeated because it did not have a unified language and ethnicity, so nationalists required a monolingual state and a reformed education curriculum (Ji, 2018, p. 70). Japan's invasion stimulated a new identity among the public. Zhao (2004, p. 106) argues that this new identity differed from foreign invaders and one's own identity, which merely cared about local affairs, and it was used for war mobilization. Moreover, nationalism presented some democratic elements. Zhong and Hwang (2020, p. 64) state that democratic movements and nationalist movements prior to 1949 in China shared ideas of national equality, national self-determination, and national liberation. Shen (2007, p. 17) defines this type of nationalism as civic nationalism, while Zhao (2004) calls it liberal nationalism, which competed with ethnic nationalism and state nationalism in the twentieth century. These nation-building attempts from intellectuals and elites continued into the post-revolutionary era.

Since the Chinese Communist Party (CCP) took the power, nationalism has presented various forms. Modongal (2016) classifies four stages of nationalism from 1949: state control nationalism (1949-1976), liberal nationalism (1979-1989), patriotic nationalism (1989-2001), and cyber-nationalism (2001-present). In the Mao era, the CCP launched measures of economic self-reliance and continuing anti-imperialism campaigns (Weatherley & Zhang, 2017, p. 18). Meanwhile, to create a multinational state, it imposed the ethnic identification project and a series of policies on the unified language. Rohsenow (2004) reviews the efforts of language policies, which included the reform of the scheme of the Pinyin system, simplification of Chinese characters, and the promotion of Mandarin from 1950s to 1970s but finds that Mao's constant political campaigns interfered and interrupted the language reform work. The state control nationalism did not work well in building an integrated country.

It kept China backward and stalled. The lack of physical mobility, economic interdependence, and powerful national literature instead strengthened regional identity and culture (Friedman, 1994). As Friedman (1994, p. 79) points out, a new national project was constructed in the 1980s with the term "Southern national narrative." In contrast to Mao's anti-imperialist nationalism, which privileged the north, inland, and peasants, the south, usually the southeastern coastal provinces, opened to market, money, mobility, and other people. Thus, he concludes that a new cultural consciousness legitimates diverse political projects, for example, a southern-based state (Friedman, 1994, p. 87).

The collapse of Mao's utopia experiment and the import of Western liberal ideas sparked a societal inclination towards learning from the West during the 1980s. This trend of Western influence permeated all levels of society, prompting a collective determination to pursue reforms. CCP improved the relations with Western countries and redirected the focus to developing a capitalist economy (Weatherley & Zhang, 2017). Intellectuals criticized traditional cultures and national character to look for alternative models (Goldman, Link, & Wei, 1993). Many publications about Western countries' history, politics, and cultures were translated and published (Modongal, 2016). People in big cities, especially Beijing and Shanghai, showed a strong need and desire to learn English (Li & Yuan, 2013). The crackdown on the Tiananmen Square movement in 1989 ended this period, and patriotic nationalism was pursued amidst the crisis of regime legitimacy in the 1990s.

CCP rediscovered the revolutionary tradition, traditional cultures, and history relics and reinterpreted them to become extensive education materials in movies, TV/radio programs, celebration activities, tourist spots, and courses in middle schools and colleges (Zhao, 2004, p. 218-223). Zhao (2004) calls this patriotic nationalism pragmatic nationalism, which includes prioritizing economic development. Modongal (2016) also adds that international factors such as the collapse of the Soviet Union, the sanctions on the crackdown on the democratic movement, the bombing of China's embassy in Belgrade, and the Hainan Island incident were the motivations for this wave of nationalism. In CCP's discourses, the Chinese nation had a glorious past but suffered the exploitation and invasion of imperial countries in the modern period. Only the CCP can revive the nation and lead it to prosperity under the constraints of limited resources, an enormous population, and an underdeveloped economy (Study Times, 2021). Accordingly, in line with the impact of the official narrative, Cabestan (2005) argues that populist nationalism arose in the latter half of the 1990s, propelled by the Taiwan Strait crisis and a series of nationalist publications. This form of nationalism is characterized by a potent anti-Western sentiment and a sense of insecurity from economic failure or social instability (Cabestan, 2005).

At the same time, the younger generation grows up with the increasing prosperity, patriotic education, and the development of internet communication technologies. The "Fen Qing" (angry youth) phenomenon came out in the 2000s. Yang and Lim (2010) define Fen Qing as the people who were born after 1980 and enjoy using the internet to articular their nationalist sentiments and sometimes also join the nationalistic movements. The sources of the anger include the psychological gap between China's expected status in the international community and actuality (Yang & Lim, 2010). Such cyber nationalism can be cosmopolitan and borderless with Chinese people studying and working abroad. Nyiri, Zhang, and Varrall (2010) find that the overseas demonstrations of the 2008 Olympics from Chinese students, young professionals, and migrants were an extension of nationalism, and the online media linked them together and formed a space to express and interact. Moreover, the imagination of a wealthier society among the younger and well-educated generation also causes filial nationalism, a new form of nationalism under deeper globalization (Fong, 2004). Fong (2004) explains young people are dissatisfied with China's flaws and low status in the world, but they identify China as a long-suffering parent and have the duty to make it wealthy and powerful by devoting capital and knowledge. Furthermore, bottom-up or grassroots nationalism evolved into more diverse and complicated forms and features over time with the pervasiveness of communication technologies and China's deepening of global participation.

For example, consumer nationalism rises with the consumption society, the booming market, and China's unfair treatment in the process of globalization. Wang (2006) defines it as an invocation of collective national identities that appears during the consumption to accept or reject material products or brand narratives from other countries. Moreover, consumer nationalism is not limited to commercial and political arenas. In fact, it relates to a spur of cultural identity among Chinese people under Westernization. As Tomlinson (2007, p. 161) explains, globalization not only creates but also threatens the "collective treasure of local communities," which need to be protected and preserved. Gao (2012) thus argues that Chinese consumers' impacts on foreign brands are expanded with the help of the internet and mobile phones, while at the macro level, the state's role is called to defend the national interest.

In addition, after the Fen Qing phenomenon, other manifestations of cyber nationalism, including the Diba Expedition launched by the members of the online fandom circle, little pinks, and the replacement theory (Ruguan Xue 入

關學)[10] emerged with new features. In particular, Diba Expedition has attracted scholars' attention to its mobilization, components, and implications (Liu, 2018; Wang, 2018; Yang, 2018). It was triggered by the Cross-Strait's conflicts on unification and independence, and the expeditioners, usually born after the 1990s, bypassed the Great Firewall to post pro-China comments under the official Facebook pages of Sanlih E-Television, Apple Daily, Liberty Times, Tsai Ing-Wen, and Ho Wan-see (Guo & Yang, 2019). Guo and Yang (2019) argue that it was a self-organized and novel nationalist movement with virtual private networks (VPNs) and memetic communication strategy. Also, the members of Expedition are called little pinks, a label that originated from "female-led, opting for soft emotional discourse of seduction and romance." Later, it referred to "broad young nationalists" (Fang & Repnikova, 2018, p. 2163). According to Fang and Repnikova (2018), the term "little pink" had little to do with female-led nationalism, but it was adopted by liberals as a means of countering allegiance to the ruling party. Also, the ruling party used the term to reinforce nationalism.

Nevertheless, in a few years, little pinks' continuation, "fangirl" comes out and presents female participation in political field (Zhuang, Huang, & Chen, 2022). Zhuang, Huang, and Chen (2022) explore the Fangirl Expedition in the protest against the Extradition Law in Hong Kong and find that the original motivation was to protect fangirls' idols who supported the Extradition Law. Amid their accidental political participation, the nation was imagined as an idol, named "Brother Ah-Zhong" (阿中哥哥), following the same logic of fandom. China, in the idolized expressions, is beautiful, strong, and innocent but suffers long-term aspersions, rumors, and stereotypes from the West. Therefore, as Brother Ah-Zhong's fans, namely China's citizens are obliged to promote and defend it (Zhuang, Huang, & Chen, 2022, p. 8-10). In short, compared with the Fen Qing generation and filial nationalists, little pinks or fangirls born after the 1990s demonstrate higher media literacy and more international experience. The Fen Qing generation and filial nationalists acknowledged the gaps between China and the developed countries. However, the post-1990 generation benefiting from China's rapid economic growth and stable environment often overestimated China's status in the world and kept confident in its development while failing to acknowledge or ignoring the internal inequality and injustice.

---

[10] The replacement theory was sourced from a user on "Zhihu" in 2019 and used in the relationship between China and America. America is viewed as the Ming dynasty while China is going to replace it as the Qing dynasty.

After President Xi Jinping came into office in 2012, the state led nationalism was upgraded to the Chinese dream under the background of economic slowdown and the uneven distribution among social classes. Compared with the American dream, the definition of the Chinese dream is vague and can be expanded. Thus, Wang (2014) argues that the Chinese dream is nothing new, and it is used to replace the CCP's previous discourses of national rejuvenation. Under the propaganda campaign, Zhao (2021) argues that Chinese nationalism has turned from affirmative to assertive through the combination of state-led nationalism and popular nationalism. A new round of patriotic education was intensified by integrating it into all level schools' courses and exams and even extending to infancy. Moreover, it attacked Western liberal values, including universal values of human rights, media independence, and civil society, and controlled the information further with a tighter Firewall (Zhao, 2021). One example of aggressiveness is the wolf warrior diplomacy. Sullivan and Wang (2022) argue that wolf warrior diplomacy is an official communication act stimulated by foreign actors' criticisms of China's positions, policies, or behaviors and interference in China's internal affairs. Wolf warrior diplomacy is spurred to serve the major-country diplomacy and fight for discursive power. Through a rude, hard, and confrontational tone viewed as strong and bold by Chinese people, it mollifies some nationalists even though the contents do not always match the state propaganda (Sullivan & Wang, 2022).

On the other hand, globalization brings segments and divisions. The rise of individualism in China legalizes the personal pursuit of happiness, pleasure, and rights (Gao, 2012). Gao (2012) points out that a growing number of mass incidents and the allowed various voices in media are the consequences. Predictably, alternative and extreme expressions can be found on the internet. Even if the aforementioned forms of grassroots or bottom-up nationalism are under the umbrella term of popular nationalism, they are not homogenous due to the multiple components from the public, commercial digital platforms, local government authorities, and state-owned enterprises (Zhang & Ma, 2023). Their performances usually deviate from the state-led nationalism narratives and challenge authoritarian politics. For example, nationalism or patriotic content become a marketing tool to make profits. Li (2018, p. 20) finds that Chinese advertisers and companies use nationalism to sell products, while, in the traffic-attracting era, patriotic content is used by influencers to attract investment and local authorities to express political loyalty (Zhang & Ma, 2023). But Zhang and Ma (2023) find that the low-quality patriotic content labeled "low-level red" or "high-level black," which is unwanted by the state, not only causes netizens' political satire but also brings trouble in diplomacy. Besides, even nationalists may not align with the pro-regime stance. Zhang, Liu, and

Wen (2018) analyzed more than 6000 microblogs of 146 opinion leaders on Weibo and found that the majority of nationalists criticized China's domestic political conditions and showed quite friendly to the so-called China's rivals. Internet nationalism thus presents diverse forms among states, majority groups, minority groups, individuals, and diaspora. Culpepper (2012) compares Chinese state nationalism and Uyghur diaspora nationalism online on Uyghur's history and culture, diaspora leadership, and Urumqi riot and argues that various parties can compete on cyber space to represent their own nationalism and influence each other's national identity. In the nationalist competition, a small diaspora's active engagement online still can challenge the regime and increase visibility in the international society (Culpepper, 2012).

Digital media and civic engagement in China

Mass media, including newspapers, radio, and television, run and funded by governments, has been positioned as the mouthpiece of CCP for a long time. Roberts (2018) finds that the media's roles in the Mao era included ideology promotion, mobilization, and education. Information was controlled firmly by the ruling party, and there was no space for private and non-state media. The internet breaks the information monopoly, and its attributes, such as lower costs, relatively free, and ampler information, have been acknowledged to help information flow and facilitate people's engagement in collective activities (Zhou, 2015). The limited availability in the real world for the public to express political opinions and influence the government makes the role of the internet and social media extremely powerful in China. Wang (2015) argues that the internet empowers individuals and the public as well as modernizes government to be more open, transparent, and responsible. Through comparing four villages' environmental collective actions in China, the successful case shows that villagers used the internet, especially mobile phones, to communicate with the local government, search for environmental protection information, and document pollution cases. Under pressure from non-government organizations and news media, the local government responded to villagers' appeals and relocated polluting factories (Wang, 2015). In the urban areas, the effects of digital media were more evident and more profound in collective actions. Liu (2019) studied seven anti-PX[11] protests in six cities in China from 2007 to 2014 and found that digital media contributes to information dissemination, participant recruitment, and opinion shaping. More importantly, new online

---

[11] PX is an abbreviation for "paraxylene", which is an organic chemical material. The PX project is often considered to carry the risk of toxicity and pollution.

tactics, for example, the PX entry on the Baidu Encyclopedia, which became participants' primary source of information during the protests, shaped public opinion and implied new repertoires of contention in Chinese society (Liu, 2019, p. 341).

Moreover, technological and socioeconomic developments generate different effects of digital media. In mainland China, popular digital media evolved with time from technology-based Web 1.0 to user-based Web 3.0, including websites, network forums, QQ, blogs, Weibo, WeChat to BiliBili, TikTok, and mobile apps. Correspondingly, people's attitudes and behaviors are changed with the attributes of media. For example, Kuang (2018, p. 125) argues that a blog provides a public space for personalized writing, which reflects a blogger's real thoughts and feelings with the disseminate, edit, comment, and exchange functions. The low threshold of public writing on a free platform makes citizen journalist possible, and the stylist writing also forms the first batch of opinion leaders on public issues. Weibo's simple, instantaneous, open, and multiple-media features make it more like a public square to discuss topics. Numerous events have been livestreamed, shared, and commented on Weibo, and many of them have received responses. The widespread saying "attention is power, circuses change China" [12] was used to praise the influence of Weibo.

On the other hand, the CCP continues to control and censor mass media and digital media in China. Initially, after market-oriented reform, the party loosened control of mass media and encouraged commercialization. In comparison to the previous role as a mouthpiece, the more commercialized media pursues higher quality content and responds to the public's needs. Within this framework, the media acts as a watchdog to make sure that domestic affairs are conducted properly (Roberts, 2018). Tai (2014) points out that at the central level, the Central Propaganda Department instructs the print media, television, and radio by fax or telephone directly on what topics to report and the ways to report, while the local censors are inclined to hide negative news reports although following the central directives.

The rise of the internet creates a bigger hole in control and censorship. In the beginning, the censorship bureaucracy was unable to react in time to unfavorable information, especially those outbreaks online, not to mention the live stream of incidents. To stimulate economic growth, internet-based media and platforms thus gain more flexibility. However, the increasing use of the internet can

---

[12] "Guan zhu jiu shi li liang, wei guan gai bian zhong guo (關注就是力量，圍觀改變中國)" stems from the commentator Xiaoshu's comment on the newspaper "Southern Weekly" in 2010.

undermine the effectiveness of traditional media. Lorentzen (2014) points out that when something out of control spreads on the internet, the authoritarian regime will decrease the mass media's freedom to report the news story. As a result, the truth behind it is not clear. After the censorship bureaucracy made more sense to govern the internet, a comprehensive online censoring system was built up. It combines software technologies such as Great Firewall, search filtering, content removal, website blocking, and the human power of internet police and online commentators (Wu & Fitzgerald, 2021).

The changes in the public sector and regulations indicate an increasing level of control and censorship on the internet in China. When the internet first appeared in 1994, the governing institution was the Ministry of Information Industry[13] which managed the infrastructure construction, information system security, and industrial development. Then, the Bureau of Internet News Regulation under the Information Office of the State Council, which exercised regulatory control over the Internet industry, was replaced by the State Internet Information Office (SIIO) to avoid poor coordination and conflicts in 2011 (Miao & Lei, 2016). SIIO's role duties included cleaning up the internet, managing online content and government online propaganda work, and investigating and punishing website-related violations (Horsley, 2022). The measures include holding regulatory talks with Weibo celebrities and nudging internet content providers to disable certain accounts (Initium Media, 2021). In 2014, it became the Cyberspace Administration of China (CAC) right under the Party's Central Cybersecurity and Informatization Leading Group headed by President Xi Jinping. In the meanwhile, the rules and laws on the internet extend to diverse fields and become more and more detailed. Miao, Jiang, and Pang (2021) find that CAC issued 47 policies in 4 years even though the Ministry of Industrial and Information Technology issued 98 policies over 24 years.

Not surprisingly, to survive and grow, internet companies and service providers in China have become a part of content censorship. For example, Sina, one of the tech giants, not only has a censorship department to monitor user content but also encourages users to report each other for untrue information (Fu, Chan, & Chau, 2013). Besides, they are required to ask for and verify users' real identity to register via identity numbers or mobile phone numbers and report illegal content to the cybersecurity and informatization departments (Shu, 2017). What's more, a few tech players dominate the digital market. BAT (Baidu, Alibaba, Tencent) occupy the most market capitalization. Users' data are stored

---

[13] It was merged into the Ministry of Industry and Information Technology in 2008. The information can be found at http://www.gov.cn/2008lh/content_921411.htm

in China under the new cybersecurity law[14], which provides an easy way to trace users behind platforms.

Nevertheless, Chinese netizens also explore different coping ways with the censorship system and the pro-government power. Their strategies to evade censorship include using VPNs to access blocked websites and adopting exchangeable keywords, word separation, homophony, images, acronyms, emojis, or satire to defeat filtering programs (Sun, 2022; Chen et al., 2023). Especially in satire, Lee (2016) summaries three types online and argues that parodic satire is most likely to survive state censorship and co-optation. Parodic satire mimics and recontextualizes the original subject's language, logic, or practice to accentuate the absurdity of a new target. For example, netizens have taken the words of the Ministry of Railways spokesman, Wang Yongping, from a press briefing where he said, "Whether or not you believe it, I believe it," and transplanted it into various situations to express their discontent. To bypass censorship, netizens also self-censor their posted content online.

Despite the widespread censorship on the Chinese internet, the awareness of censorship can serve as an incentive for netizens to seek out information and take action. The White Paper movement, which was considered the most widespread and open protest after the Tiananmen Square movement, is the best example. It erupted by a fire in Urumqi with the doubts and critics of Covid restrictions and soon developed a wave of protests in a dozen cities (Che & Chien, 2022). A blank sheet of paper became the movement icon, and the videos of holding white papers in demonstrations went viral in and beyond Chinese social media. Predictably, the videos and pictures of protests were highly censored on the Chinese internet, but netizens adopted some tactics to circumvent censorship, such as re-recorded videos, rotated videos on their sides, stored data on Twitter and Instagram (Rosen, 2022). Eventually, the movement not only changed the central government's lockdown policy but also encouraged overseas anti-regime force. A number of public accounts on Twitter, Instagram, Telegram, and civil organizations were set up during the lockdown period (Chen, 2023).

Given the above, the promotion of a national language can restrict the development of dialects and is often used by the state to unify the population and promote nationalism. Changes in the national language policy are closely

---

[14] The Cybersecurity Law of the People's Republic of China. Retrieved at https://digichina.stanford.edu/work/translation-cybersecurity-law-of-the-peoples-republic-of-china-effective-june-1-2017/

linked to the development of state nationalism. The declining status of Cantonese in China, on the one hand, has been aware of by the residents. On the other hand, its space is being curbed further by nationalism along with the rise of China. However, the internet empowers grassroots and provides new space for dialects to grow under restrictions and handicaps. Considering Cantonese influence on cultural works and the global speaking population, its situation is likely to be more complex. The book continues the conversation.

Research design and methods

This section introduces the research design and the methods. To answer the research questions, eight typical and well-known cases about Cantonese people and Cantonese cultures are chosen after long-term observation on the Chinese internet. They are one TV program broadcasted at the local TV station in Guangzhou, three talk shows on social media, two Cantonese discussion forums, and two Facebook groups made or shared by Cantonese speakers within and beyond China. Notably, the chosen cases do not focus on language teaching and learning since the book does not approach Cantonese from a linguistic perspective.

Despite Facebook not being the primary social media platform in mainland China, the extensive use of Cantonese beyond China's borders and the global presence of Cantonese communities make it difficult to disregard its significance. In essence, while the Baidu Cantonese forum primarily attracts prominent Cantonese speakers, Facebook boasts a considerable number of Cantonese users within China. Additionally, Facebook hosts a wider array of opinions, ranging from diverse to extreme, compared to the Baidu Forum.

Table 0.1 lists the names, slogans, platforms, and number of followers for eight cases, which are presented in Chinese and Cantonese. The book provides translations for their names, introductions, episodes, and posted contents, except for the titles of "Canton One Two" and "Crazy Canton," which are cited in English. Also, eight cases exhibit diverse features due to their media attributes. Based on the extent of flexibility and interaction, the TV show has the least amount of flexibility and interaction despite adding a Quick Response Code on the TV screen for audience participation. The four discussion groups on forums and Facebook are in the middle of the ranking, offering multiple functions provided by their respective platforms. Lastly, the three talk shows on social media have the highest level of flexibility and instant interaction, allowing for the cocreation of agendas between producers and viewers.

Table 0.1: Eight Chosen Cases about Cantonese People and Cantonese Cultures[15]

Case	Slogan/Introduction	Platform	Followers
粵知一二 Canton One Two	Create Cantonese New Popularity	Tik Tok, WeChat, YouTube, Facebook Weibo, BiliBili	12086K[16] 162K 3253K
瘋狂粵語 Crazy Canton	There were stories	BiliBili YouTube	116K[17] 206K
誰語爭鋒 Language Hero	Show Dialects Win Awards	TV program Facebook, YouTube	/
粵语卜卜斋 Cantonese Buk Buk Zaai	a breath of fresh air in Cantonese cultural circle	BiliBili, WeChat, Weibo, Tik Tok	331K[18] 260K
粵語吧 Jyut Jyu Baa	the platform for Cantonese discussion, learning, and research	Baidu Tieba	279K
廣東話吧 Gwong Dung Waa Baa	the gathering zone of Cantonese lovers	Baidu Tieba	24K
廣州人 Gwong Zau Jan	We support local cultures and encourage you to write in Cantonese	Facebook	4.7K
粵人粵語~廣府語言文化復興園區 Cantonese Revival Zone	big family of ethnic Cantonese around the world	Facebook	0.9 K

The TV program "Language Hero" aims at facilitating interactions among the dialects and languages spoken in Guangdong, including Hakka, Teochew, and Taishanese dialects during 2014-2018. While three talk shows, "Canton One Two, Crazy Canton, and Cantonese Buk Buk Zaai," are run by Cantonese speakers in Guangdong on multiple online platforms. They still exist and continue to attract fans and followers, except that the show "Crazy Canton" has ended in 2017. The two discussion forums of Baidu about the news, usages, and

---

[15] Their weblinks can be found here:

Canton One Two https://space.bilibili.com/95515699; Crazy Canton https://space.bilibili.com/23080377/video; Language Hero https://www.gdtv.cn/tvColumnVideo/857; Cantonese Buk Buk Zaai https://space.bilibili.com/49637627/video; Jyut Jyu Baa https://reurl.cc/1opR4m; Gwong Dung Waa Baa https://reurl.cc/2ovLnn; Gwong Zau Jan https://www.facebook.com/groups/1501040153535706; Cantonese Revival Zone https://www.facebook.com/groups/2234732140147209.

[16] Canton One Two runs multiple channels so the table only lists the number of followers on Tik Tok (12086K), YouTube (162K), and Bili Bili (3253K).

[17] Crazy Canton has stopped updating so the table records the largest number on Bili Bili (116K) and YouTube (206K) in history.

[18] Cantonese Buk Buk Zaai mainly runs three accounts, and the table lists the number of followers on Bili Bili (331K) and Tik Tok (260K).

events of Cantonese are "Jyut Jyu Baa" and "Gwong Dung Waa Baa." The last are two Facebook groups, "Gwong Zau Jan" and "Cantonese Revival Zone," which, in fact, gather Cantonese lovers in and beyond Guangdong, so the analyzed posts are the ones about Cantonese people and written in Cantonese.

In order to understand the current situation of Cantonese in Guangdong and the meaning behind the shows and posts, the book also invites five interviewees to conduct the research. Table 0.2 lists their names and positions. They are one producer of the talk show "Cantonese Buk Buk Zaai," one administrator of the Facebook group "Gwong Zau Jan," one director of the TV program "Language Hero," one activist in Guangzhou, and one media worker and researcher of Cantonese cultures. Among five interviewees, they all can speak Cantonese, and four were born and grew up in Guangdong. Buk Zai and Tony Li in the table are nick names.

Table 0.2: The list of the interviewees

Name	Position
Lao, Zhenyu	activist, the founder of Gznf.net (羊城網)
Buk Zai	the producer of "Cantonese Buk Buk Zaai"
Li, Tony	the administrator of Facebook group "Gwong Zau Jan"
Huang, Jingyu	the director of the TV show "Language Hero"
Rao Yuansheng	media worker, the researcher of Cantonese cultures

Considering the features of cases and the research purpose, the book employs document analysis, case studies, semi-structured interviews, and content analysis to understand and analyze data. Document analysis is a method of analyzing various documents, including books, newspaper articles, journal articles, and institutional reports (Morgan, 2022). To elicit meaning, gain understanding, and develop empirical knowledge, it also combines with other research methods (Bowen, 2009). Given the background information and the tracking of changes provided by the documents, the book uses laws, policies, and official records to outline the development of the national language in the first chapter.

A case study is usually a qualitative method with a small number of cases and particular evidence to help explain larger classes of cases (Gerring, 2011). It is an intensive study with observations and cases (Skarbek, 2020). An observation includes several measured dimensions that influence a case, and a case study should have more than one observation (Gerring, 2006). Hence, a good case study should be one case or a small number of cases with many observations.

Aside from analyzing cases, an interview helps to understand the stories behind them. The method of interview includes structured, semi-structured, and unstructured interviews. Semi-structured interview combines structured and unstructured interviews by asking questions under a predetermined questions list, which is to guide the interviewer (Doyle, 2022). George (2022) argues that the question order and the number of questions are flexible. Since the questions are open-ended, the method usually fits an explore study. Its conducting procedure includes setting a goal, designing questions, choosing participants, confirming the medium, conducting the interview, and analyzing interviews (George, 2022). In this book, four interviewees are located in Guangdong, and one interviewee lives in New York, so the online interview without showing faces and email are the ways to collect data. Also, five interviews were conducted separately from 2021-2022, and each took around one hour. In the interview with Tony Li, a supplementary interview was added after the first interview.

Content analysis as a research method was first used in the communication field by counting the frequency of certain words or phrases' appearances in written, verbal, or visual messages. It can be an objective mean with a set of procedures of conceptualization, unitization, sampling, and operationalization (Fico, Lacy, & Riffe, 2008) or a subjective mean as a part of textual analysis by personal categorizing (Bainbridge, 2011). Usually, similar words or phrases are classified in the same category. At the preparation stage, according to the research question, the researcher decides the unit of analysis, which can be a letter, a word, a sentence, or the number of participants (Elo & Kyngäs, 2008). Elo and Kyngäs (2008, p. 109) argue that the researcher analyzes the chosen content based on the research purpose and reads it thoroughly enough in advanced to get the most from the data. Nowadays, the analyzed data is not limited to the complete and well-organized text, as adopting electronic and dynamic data has become popular in various research (Lacy et al., 2015). As a result, the internet data becomes the analyzed text. As the book's samples, each episode of the TV and talk shows and each post on the forums and in Facebook groups are the units of analysis. It needs to be pointed out that the data online is dynamic and restricted to time and context. Thus, the initially collected data in the book may have new changes.

Chapter 1

History and Government Policies of Cantonese and Mandarin

Mandarin was not inherently destined to become the national language, and Cantonese did not initially exist as a dialect. According to linguistic definitions, Mandarin and Cantonese are distinct languages due to their lack of mutual intelligibility. However, in mainland China, non-official languages are often categorized as dialects, irrespective of their mutual comprehensibility. Therefore, it is necessary to examine the relationships between Cantonese and Mandarin. Otherwise, people cannot understand why Cantonese is insisted on by Cantonese speakers and why the creations online are so productive and influential. Additionally, shifts in the status of Mandarin reflect the changing circumstances of Cantonese. Thus, this chapter sheds light on the development of both languages in China.

A unified script has a very long history in China. However, before a nation state appeared, there was no national language but the common tongue (Tong Yong Yu 通用語). In ancient China, it is called Yayan (雅言) language, but Ci (2015) argues that Mandarin (Guanhua 官話) based on the northern dialects around Beijing already appeared at the end of the Ming dynasty (1368-1644). It was used by the central and regional governors and prevailed in the north and the novels of colloquial Chinese (Li, 2011). Coupled with intellectuals' efforts on enlightenment writing, the popularity of common tongue increased. Still, in the south region, dialects were dominant.

Cantonese oral and writing tradition

It is said that Cantonese originates from the integrations between the Yayan language from the Central Plains and the local Yue language (越語)[1] during the Qin and Han dynasties (Huang, 2021). However, Li Xinkui (1994, p. 44) opposes this popular opinion and argues that its source can be traced back to the Chu language spoken by Chu people because Lingnan (嶺南)[2] was ruled by the Chu State in the Warring States Period (476BC-221BC). Although there are different

---

[1] Yue (越) means water or ocean. Yue people (越人) refer to the people live by the sea.

[2] Lingnan refers to the region in the south of five mountains. It included Guangdong, Guangxi, Hainan, Hong Kong, Macau, and a small part of Vietnam in history.

opinions on Cantonese origins, it is widely believed that Cantonese as a historical language retains many of the ancient Chinese language's phonological, lexical, and syntactic elements. Compared with Mandarin's four tones, its nine sounds and six tones are closer to ancient pronunciation and more suitable for reading Tang poetry (Li, 2017; Chiu, 2020).

Cantonese is well-known for oral expression in daily communication and entertainment industries, but Li Yuen Mei (2011, p. 21) finds that Cantonese as a written language was published at the end of the Ming dynasty. It first appeared in the genres of songs such as the southern songs (Naam Yam 南音), wooden fish songs (Muk Jyu Go 木魚歌), and love songs (Jyut Au 粵謳), then it developed into multiple genres of literature since late Qing dynasty (Snow, 2013). In other words, unlike most dialects in China, Cantonese has its own written form. As Bauer (2018, p. 113) points out, Cantonese can be written with standard Chinese characters, Cantonese characters, English alphabet, and the empty box "□" for the lack of a Chinese character. Aside from the literature for entertainment and leisure, Cantonese textbooks, newspapers, and revolutionary propaganda also came out to disseminate new ideas of state and institution (Ching, 2006). Moreover, missionaries' Cantonese writing in Guangdong is another phenomenon to be reckoned with. To promote religions to the public, missionaries learned Mandarin and Cantonese but chose to write Cantonese in religious publications and dictionaries as it was used by most people (Li, 2011). Cantonese writing, pronunciation, usage, translation, and even the social realities of their time were recorded. Both Li (2011) and Ching (2006) argue that it was the collections and organization made by missionaries that paved the way for standardized Cantonese Pinyin (Jyutping 粵拼) and writing. Local operas also pushed Cantonese vernacular development after they performed in oral Cantonese and wrote scripts in written Cantonese since the 1930s (Zheng, 2015).

Mandarin as national language

As has already been pointed out before, nationalists embraced nationalism to save the nation, so some attempts to reform and unify the verbal and written language were adopted by the Qing government in the program of teaching Mandarin at schools in 1909 (Ji, 2018). However, this effort was short-lived as the Qing government was soon overthrown, along with the intention of calling Mandarin the national language (Ci, 2015). The successor to the Qing government, the Republican government, further confirmed Mandarin as a national language with the national language movement. It started with the unification of pronunciation by convening a commission and eventually confirmed the Beijing dialect as the standard sound (De Francis, 1950). The consensus was not easy to reach under the diverse views on language and the disputes from Southern representatives at conferences. Dialects and foreign languages still had a strong existence during the republican period (1912-1949). Ci (2015) uses the Nationalist Party's second national congress as an example to prove that Cantonese was used as a weapon to fight for power. Also, in the left-wing intellectuals' movements of Latinization, dialects were encouraged in literature and movie creation, and their definition of a national language or Putonghua was the integration of dialects (Ci, 2015). Besides, Zhao (2018) finds that foreign languages such as German, French, English, and Japanese could be found in many writers' Chinese modern novels.

To promote Mandarin and increase literacy, the measures under the Republican government included the publication of dictionaries and the issuing of orders to teach the phonetic alphabet at schools (Ji, 2018, p. 71; De Francis, 1950, p. 60). In addition, the advocacy of script reform rose with the Baihua (plain language) movement, which suggested the alphabetical writing or the simplification of Chinese characters. Wan (2014) argues that the Romanization of Chinese can be traced back to missionaries' practices in the costal regions, and these advocacies in the 1930s were based on the premise that Chinese traditional writing systems are backward. In all, the Republican government's language policies were not effective. On the one hand, the government lacked the authority to enact. On the other hand, the country was faced with separatist movements and foreign invasions. Nonetheless, those measures were inherited by the CCP.

The struggles between Cantonese and Mandarin in the People's Republic of China

After the CCP gained power in 1949, Mandarin continued to be adopted as the national speech, which was officially confirmed in 1956. CCP first launched a campaign and established a committee to promote Mandarin and eradicate illiteracy in the 1950s (Luqiu, 2018). Lam (2008) summarizes two main approaches: the simplification of the writing script and the development of Hanyu Pinyin. From 1956, the explicit measures included teaching Mandarin in all schools in Han Chinese regions, training teachers in workshops, introducing the Pinyin form of pronunciation, and simplifying script characters (Lam, 2005; Ji, 2018). These measures in Han Chinese regions were not innovative, but for minority languages, the CCP followed the Soviet linguistic model to standardize 16 minority nationalities' languages and reform or create their writing systems as well (Zhou, 2011).

The goal of modernization and Mandarin's official status necessitate an examination of the relationships between Mandarin and dialects. The new regime rejected the definition of Putonghua among the left-wing intellectuals in the 1930s (Ci, 2015) and viewed dialects as obstacles to modernization at the early stage (Guo, 2004). CCP's official newspaper, the People's Daily first stated that "Mandarin is for all people, and dialects are for the people of a region...the spread of Mandarin does not mean the artificial elimination of dialects, but only the gradual reduction of their scope of use... dialects can and definitely will coexist with Mandarin for a long period of time, but we must continue to expand the scope of Mandarin" (The People's Daily, 1955). The statement caused the popular concern that dialects would naturally die out if not forced out (Guo, 2004). Hence, to help promote Mandarin, Premier Zhou Enlai declared in the report "The current task of script reform" that "promoting Mandarin is to remove gaps among dialects not banning or eliminating them...dialects will exist for a long time" (Zhou, 1958).

Even though the campaign promoting Mandarin was ongoing within the country, dialects were tolerated due to the small number of educated people who could train or teach Mandarin and the lack of mobility between city and town (Ip, 2010). In Guangdong, Ci (2015) points out that the value of Cantonese in united front work helped Cantonese operas, plays, and movies continue to develop, and even in the provincial government and schools, the resistance to use Mandarin was strong. After the stagnation during the Cultural Revolution (1966-1976), the Mandarin promotion activity bounced back, and Mandarin as the official language was confirmed by the Constitution in 1982 (Ci, 2015). In response, laws, policies, and regulations required the public arenas, such as schools, workplaces, and mass media to use Mandarin in the 1980s. In addition, a new goal was set at the National Conference on Language and Script in 1986 to make Mandarin the instructional language in all schools, the working language in government, the language for radio and television broadcasting, cinemas, and theaters, and even the lingua franca among speakers of various local dialects by the end of the twentieth century (Zhang & Guo, 2012).

The Guangdong government also released notices [3] to echo the central government's language policies. However, for Cantonese in the 1980s, it was a golden age due to the decentralization of economic management and decision-making. Guangdong, like other coastal regions, was encouraged to use the comparative advantage of its geo-political locations, for example, the relationship with Hongkong, for trade, technology transfer, and investment with the outside world during the economic transition (Goodman, 1994). Moreover, overseas Chinese who are of Guangdong origins throughout Southeast Asia, Australia, and North America donated to build public facilities and invested in industries in hometowns (Goodman & Feng, 1994, p. 180).

---

[3] The notices in 1981 and 1982 can be found at

http://www.gd.gov.cn/zwgk/gongbao/1981/4/content/post_3353799.html
http://www.gd.gov.cn/zwgk/gongbao/1982/3/content/post_3353968.html

Benefiting from the reform and opening up policy, Guangdong became not only the most vibrant hub of trade and export but also the trendsetter of popular culture. New fashions such as music teahouses, bands, pop songs, and ballroom dancing first appeared in Guangdong (Hu, 2018), and Hong Kong's cultural products also spread across the border. To watch Hong Kong's TV programs directly, the residents of Guangdong ignored the ban and installed antennae at home (Ho & Lu, 2019). Since Cantonese is the dominant language in Guangdong and Hong Kong, non-Cantonese speaking migrant workers had to learn Cantonese to live and work (Yue, 2023).

One noticeable example of Cantonese impact on China is that Cantonese as a Southern dialect has introduced or created large numbers of new, modern, and functional words and expressions in life and economy for the first time. According to statistics, the total number has been more than 600 (Tang, 2005). These new words included the precious clothes material "Dik Kok Loeng" (的確涼) translated from Dacron, imported from Guangzhou in the 1970s, "Sir" (先生) "Miss" (小姐), which replaced "Tong Zhi" (comrade 同志) between strangers, the "Saan Zaai" (copy 山寨) culture, and the recent "Hou Sai Lei" (amazing 猴賽雷/好犀利) and "Gong Zan" (honestly 港真). Cantonese made crucial contributions to introducing new things and activating cultures for Chinese people.

Economic success and further market-oriented transition raised regional autonomy and the media's capacity to negotiate with regulators. Aside from Cantonese, other dialects' TV programs from the provincial to county levels revived in the 1990s with the genres of news, dramas, films, sitcoms, variety shows, and talk shows (Zhang & Guo, 2012). Zhang and Guo (2012) argue that dialect TV programs not only challenge the hegemony of Mandarin but also shake the hegemonic national Chinese identity by nurturing local identity. Ji (2018, p. 78) also finds that local officers did not actively implement the Mandarin promotion policy due to the profits generated by dialect programs of local media.

However, this does not mean the governor allowed and encouraged dialect revival. The State Language Commission identified Guangdong, Fujian, and Shanghai as the priority areas for the promotion of Mandarin in the southern areas in 1991 (Liu, 1993). One year later, the Guangdong government issued a decision that Mandarin, not Cantonese, should be the standard language of the province by using it as the working language of public service sectors by the end of 1994, the language of instruction in all schools by the end of 1995 and frequent broadcasting language of radio and television stations (Chen, 1999, p. 59). At the national level, a standardized Mandarin test called the Putonghua Proficiency Test was established to improve pronunciation skills and set requirements for certain professionals, including public servants, teachers, and broadcasters (Saillard, 2004, p. 166). Although Guo (2004, p. 49) argues that language planners and scholars rediscovered the meaning of dialects and had new views of the relationships between Mandarin and dialects in the 1990s, there was a constant negotiation between local broadcasters and regulators. Zhuang (2016) finds that the National Radio and Television Administration has been issuing regulations to restrict dialects from 2000 to 2009 while dialect TV and radio programs kept growing at the same time. After 2000, the specialized law of the standard spoken and written Chinese language[4] came out to identify Mandarin's usage and status, and it also stipulated the situational usage scopes of dialects, such as broadcasting under approval, the needs in traditional arts, research, publishing, and official business. In the policy implementation of Guangdong, Ho and Lu (2019) found that Cantonese was still allowed during class breaks and during activity time at schools in the 1990s, but it was forbidden at all times, even at the kindergarten level, after mid-2000.

Mandarin's dominant status has gradually affected the language preferences and attitudes of Chinese people. With the powerful promotion and universal application in everyday life, speaking Mandarin provides the convenience of oral communication nationwide but also indicates privilege, at least in cultural and career development. The success of Mandarin promotion is so impressive that more than 80% of the Chinese population can speak Mandarin (Zhao & Wu, 2020), while more and more parents choose not to communicate with their children with dialects at home (Zhao, 2019). Dialects in practice are discouraged or even banned by regional governments in public spheres, although no laws claim to eliminate them (Luqiu, 2018; Ng & Zhao, 2015). Compared with the Cantonese golden age, current migrant workers lose incentives to learn Cantonese, and local Cantonese speakers switch to speak Mandarin with Mandarin-speaking migrants.

Moreover, the Chinese government pushes for Mandarin's international development. From providing short-term and long-term immersion programs for international students in China to establishing Confucius Institutes in foreign universities and Confucius Classrooms in foreign schools, Mandarin becomes a foreign language (Feng & Adamson, 2019). Similar to the Putonghua Proficiency Test within China, an assessment scheme (Hanyu Shuiping Kaoshi) for non Chinese speakers who want to study or work in China was also set up in 1992 and has developed into an international standard (Ministry of Education, 1992).

---

[4] Law of the People's Republic of China on the Standard Spoken and Written Chinese Language at http://www.gov.cn/ziliao/flfg/2005-08/31/content_27920.htm

In the Xi Jinping era, the campaign of Mandarin promotion has been reinforced. For example, the Putonghua Proficiency Test, which was initially designed for professionals, has been extended to elementary school students since 2022 (Wu, 2022). Under the name of dialect protection and traditional cultures promotion, the central government launched a big digital project (Zhongguo Yuyan Ziyuan Baohu Gongcheng 中國語言資源保護工程)[5] in 2015 by collecting and recording lexical and syllabic data with texts, pictures, sounds, and videos as well. The first five-year phase of the project has concluded, but its impact remains uncertain due to ongoing concerns from netizens about the preservation of dialects in cyberspace. Therefore, Zhou (2018, p. 77-78) points out that the supremacy of Putonghua in mainland China is unassailable, and citizens have no intention to challenge it. Furthermore, he posits that dialects, in general, are regarded as cultural heritage rather than living languages. Simultaneously, certain ethnic groups' language rights are challenged under the new language policy. In contrast to the dialects in Han people regions, minority languages have been being protected by laws since 1949. Minorities have the right to preserve and develop their languages and scripts in the constitution and the Law on Regional National Autonomy (Ji, 2018, p. 82). However, recent measures revealed a paradox. Bilingual education in practice became Mandarin education in Xinjiang and Tibet (Hoshur, 2021; Wu, 2020). Mandarin started to replace Mongolian as the teaching language of three subjects in elementary and middle schools in 2020 in the Inner Mongolia Autonomous Region (Gan, 2020), while the only Mongolian social media "Bainu" with 400 thousand users in China was shut down (Chen, 2020).

Regarding Cantonese, it is still useful for unification in serving the central government's ongoing Greater Bay Area project,[6] a regional development plan to further integrate Hong Kong, Macau, and Guangdong since 2019. Nevertheless, according to the official report of the language in this area, the status of Mandarin and simplified Chinese (Jian Ti Zhong Wen 簡體中文) is highlighted by the actions of testing and teaching in Hong Kong where Cantonese and traditional Chinese (Fan Ti Zhong Wen 繁體中文) are used formally even if English and Portuguese are also mentioned to get trained for the "One Belt One Road" program (Ministry of Education, 2021). On the other hand, beyond the official intentions, there are practices and discourses of Cantonese protection and promotion from non-state actors. A differentiating trend is that a pan-Cantonese identity is being constructed with written

---

[5] The project can be found at https://zhongguoyuyan.cn/index

[6] The project includes Guangzhou, Shenzhen, Foshan, Zhuhai, Zhongshan, Dongguan, Jiangmen, Huizhou, Zhaoqing, Hong Kong and Macau up to 11 cities in the Pearl River Delta region.

Cantonese on the internet (Carrico, 2012). Based on these assumptions, Carrico (2012, p. 40) finds that Guangdong's economic power and Cantonese cultural heritage underpin a new value and even nationality against the Han unity and state nationalism.

To sum up, Cantonese and Mandarin are not equal in status. The influence of Cantonese depends more on history, including the diaspora and economic power, while Mandarin's relies more on political power. Dialects in China are usually viewed as traditional cultures to be inherited and protected, but the CCP seems to pay lip-service only. When the central government or the regime is weak, dialects are tolerated and utilized to meet the goal. Once the central is strong, the national language is expected to become a lingua franca among multiple nations. It can be said that the process of promoting Mandarin in China is the power struggle between the central and local. The fate of Cantonese is thus determined by China's economy and local power.

Chapter 2
Dominant Cantonese and Diverse Dialects in Guangdong

Generally, Cantonese is translated in Chinese as Gwong Dung Waa (廣東話) or Jyut Jyu (粵語), signifying "the language of Guangdong."[1] Among the various variants of Cantonese, the standard form is usually known as "Gwong Zau Waa" (Guangzhou dialect 廣州話). Nevertheless, Cantonese is not the sole language spoken by the inhabitants of this region. Beyond Cantonese, other dialects or languages that lack mutual intelligibility also thrive in Guangdong. According to Chang and Zhuang (2008), there are mainly three dialects (Jyut 粵, Min 閩, Hakka 客家) under the Chinese language family and one Shaozhou Tuhua (韶州土話). It is said that the Cantonese-speaking population is estimated at 40 million, while the Hakka-speaking population comprises 20 million, and the Min-speaking population totals 17 million within Guangdong (The Paper, 2019). In other words, it is common that the inhabitants who were born and raised outside the Pearl River Delta region do not speak Cantonese.

Discussing Guangdong and the perception of its people inevitably involves the presence of diverse ethnic groups and their respective dialects or languages. The chapter starts with the local TV show "Language Hero" to explain the unequal status between Cantonese and other dialects in Guangdong. Their relationship is similar to the one between Cantonese and Mandarin, albeit without official documentation to delineate it. The predominance of Cantonese is primarily attributed to economic and cultural growth rather than political factors.

Language Hero

As a language contest, "Language Hero" introduced and educated viewers about the history and knowledge of the dialects in Guangdong. For the first

---

[1] People from different Cantonese-speaking regions use different names to call Cantonese: Gwong Dung Waa (廣東話), Jyut Jyu (粵語), Baak Waa (白話), Gwong Zau Waa (廣州話), Gwong Fu Waa (廣府話), and Tong Waa (唐話).

time, the show brought together different dialects spoken in twenty cities[2], presenting them on traditional media. According to the director Huang Jingyu, it was inspired by the show of Hunan Television, which is famous for entertainment programs in China. Also, Guangdong's various dialects and languages supported the show's creations, although the broadcasting was helpful to promote Cantonese.

Figure 2.1: The poster of Language Hero Season 4

Note. The screenshot is captured from the show's official website.
Source: https://www.gdtv.cn/tvColumnVideo/857

TVS, as the first dialect satellite channel in mainland China, broadcasts its TV programs in Cantonese. As Figure 2.1 shows, two local male hosts were in charge of the program. They introduced the rules, participants, and experts in Cantonese and activated the atmosphere. In accordance with Huang Jingyu, "Language Hero" was the first variety show of the TVS and was designed in 2013. In the show, the ways of competition were not the same in four seasons, but the focus was always on the dialects of 20 cities. It is important to note that even though the show presented the dialects along with the administrative boundaries of cities, their connections are more complex and multilayered. Cantonese is the common language in 9 cities of the Pearl River Delta region, but it differs in pronunciation and meaning to some degree; Meizhou collects

---

[2] Guangdong is divided into 21 cities: Guangzhou, Foshan, Zhaoqing, Shenzhen, Jiangmen, Zhuhai, Huizhou, Zhongshan, Chaozhou, Shantou, Shanwei, Jieyang, Heyuan, Meizhou, Dongguan, Yunfu, Zhanjiang, Yangjiang, Maoming, Shaoguan, Qingyuan. Shenzhen is composed of migrants, so it was not included in the show.

Dominant Cantonese and Diverse Dialects

the most Hakka people, while the Hakka dialect is also spoken in Heyuan and some areas of the Pearl River Delta region; Teochew dialect is shared in the Chaoshan (潮州汕頭) region of the East Guangdong; Jyut, Min, and Hakka dialects can be found in Zhanjiang.

The theme song of the show reflects the complexity of the dialects. Figure 2.2 is the screenshot of the 4-minute theme song, which combines at least 20 dialects sung by the hosts from 20 TV stations. It is a rap with local accents about a brief introduction of 20 cities and starts with Cantonese/Gwong Zau Waa (Guangzhou dialect 廣州話). Each host sings 4 pieces of lyrics. In particular, the part of Maoming city includes 4 accents of 3 local county-level cities (Jian Liu, 2016). A non-Cantonese speaker may not find the disparities of these dialects, but a Cantonese speaker can hear the differences in the song. As the picture shows, the host, Pan Weifen, from Shaoguan, is Yao nationality (Yaozu 瑤族), one of the 55 officially recognized ethnic minorities who basically gathers in certain counties under Shaoguan and Qingyuan city. The Yao language (瑤話) is not mutually intelligible with Cantonese.

Figure 2.2: The theme song of the show

Note. The merged screenshot is captured from YouTube. Source: https://www.youtube.com/watch?v=u53FCoAsdoo

Since the show's focus was dialects, its target audience should be the native people of Guangdong. To Cantonese speakers, watching the show can be a challenge because the show refers to the dialects that they barely know, let alone the Mandarin speakers. Moreover, even the migrants who know Cantonese still do not understand the contexts behind the dialects. In short, it was not a language teaching TV program but displayed the multi-language and multicultural facet of Guangdong by incorporating life elements.

The production team took great care in preparing the questions for the contest, as they consulted with experts about the usages, meanings, and history of the dialects in the 20 cities featured on the show. In the first season, participants were recruited as teams composed of five members, and in the second season, the participants became celebrities from 20 cities which represented 20 dialects. Then, the participants in the third season turned to individuals in each episode to fight for the champion. To attract a larger audience, Season 4 invited well-known hosts, actors, and singers from Hong Kong and Guangdong to lead the recruited teams.

Figure 2.3 shows the general components of the show. The hosts stood in the middle of the stage, and the participants sat on the left side to answer questions. Sometimes, they moved to the middle to finish drawing or eating tasks. On the right side, the hosts from 20 television stations asked questions in an oral or acting way. The recreated pictures, music, videos, movies, and dramas were used as the testing materials. Also, 2-3 experts from local universities sat beside the hosts and were invited to explain answers.

Figure 2.3: Episode 1 of Season 2

Note. The screenshot is captured from 56.com. Source: https://www.56.com/u19/v_MTM4Njg2MzM2.html

Dominant Cantonese and Diverse Dialects

Speaking of the design of the show, it did not have a coherent theme alone with four seasons. Thus, it is hard to summarize the main content. The sections of the competition were also flexible, and the ways of the test for participants were various. Figure 2.4 shows one of the most popular games in game shows. The questioners on the right side proposed the ideas or concepts in dialects, and then the first team member expressed the core contents in Cantonese or dialects with postures to the next teammate. The last team member guessed and explained the meaning. No matter under what name the testing styles were, the purpose was to know about the dialects in Guangdong.

Figure 2.4: The Episode 1 of Season 4

Note. The screenshot is captured from its official website.
Source: https://www.gdtv.cn/tvColumnVideo/857

The example of the phrase "stealing vegetable" (Tau Coi 偷菜) presented the characteristics of the show. The host from Zhuhai asked participants questions about the custom of seeking romantic relationships in the Doumen area in Cantonese and Doumen dialect. Then, the participants guessed the meaning in Cantonese. After the answer was announced, the expert explained the answer in dialect and Mandarin. Tau Coi is a traditional activity on the thirteenth day of the first lunar month where young girls who look for good partners go to someone's vegetable garden sneakily to steal a vegetable. This blessing activity has lasted for 200 years, so it is encouraged by the local people. Similarly, Tau Coi also exists in the areas of Yangjiang and Shanwei. In this example, several languages or dialects were spoken or heard at the same time. Tau Coi as a custom shared in some areas of Guangdong, even though its meaning and forms vary.

Therefore, participants with multi-cultural backgrounds or multiple regional experiences are more likely to win the show. It is worth noting that all the participants who made it to the final round of the competition in the four seasons were born and raised in the Guangdong area for over 30 years. If they joined the show as a team, a common component was that five members were from five cities of Guangdong. To those who joined as one person or duo, the experience became more important. For example, in Season 3, one of the top local TV hosts, Ren Yongquan, born in 1968, and his daughter defeated two local actors to win the show.

In all, the shapes and accents of the dialects in Guangdong are much more than the summarized 20 categories. To the non Guangdong audience, the show presented the look of multiple languages and cultures in Guangdong. To the Guangdong audience, it built a virtual world to reach and communicate with the weaker dialects, which are often invisible in public. To both Guangdong and non Guangdong audiences, the show brings up the variants of the Cantonese language family, which are with local accents and somewhat cannot communicate with each other. As Gao (2015) contends, diverse languages in China usually mean potential conflicts and threats to political unity. Cantonese and other dialects in Guangdong are not exceptions. In addition to the historical conflicts among the three groups, some contemporary Cantonese speakers belittle and devalue those variants of Cantonese with the view that they are not standard or original Cantonese, which often causes disputes of language divisions and identity conflicts among Cantonese people. In the heyday of Cantonese, another two subgroups, namely Hakka people and Teochew people, learned Cantonese while Cantonese also incorporated vocabulary from Hakka and Teochew dialects. However, nowadays, Mandarin has become the primary tool of communication among three groups.

The alterations of game rules within the show serve as reflections of Cantonese's dominant status. In the preceding three seasons, all game types revolved around the dialects of 19 cities, excluding Cantonese/Gwong Zau Waa. However, the addition of the segments "Cantonese Solitaire" and "Cantonese XO" in Season Four, presented in Gwong Zau Waa, diminished the prominence of other dialects. The rationale behind these changes, as stated by the director, was to boost viewership. Consequently, dialects or languages from other regions within Guangdong on a Cantonese-speaking TV channel received limited exposure. In response to these shifts in the game's format, Huang Jingyu calmly predicts that the decline of dialects is inevitable, even though the TV station continues to produce Cantonese programs. Moreover, based on her knowledge, there are no plans to create new dialect-based shows in the future, suggesting an unalterable trend.

Chapter 3

The Image of Cantonese People and The Censorship Online

Language conveys thoughts and identity. It is usually viewed as a mean to identify membership with its boundary function (Tabouret-Keller, 1998). Following Chapter 2's introduction of the dialectal and linguistic landscape of Guangdong via a TV show, this chapter employs three social media talk shows to highlight the characteristics of Cantonese and the collective identity it represents. Additionally, the chapter delves into an analysis of censorship and self-censorship encompassing governmental bodies, commercial platforms, and content creators. In contrast to television content, the shows on social media evoke a greater range of ideas and prompt immediate reactions, but they also entail heightened operational risks.

Cantonese Buk Buk Zaai

The team of the "Cantonese Buk Buk Zaai" comprises only two individuals, posing challenges in establishing an efficient production system. The infrequent online releases often prompt jests from its fan base, who humorously comment with phrases like "the missing person comes back" on the screen. Furthermore, the show's themes maintain a rather informal nature. The producer, Buk Zai, takes charge of selecting topics, crafting scripts, and providing voiceovers for the show, while the second team member is responsible for creating animations.

Figure 3.1: The homepage of the "Cantonese Buk Buk Zaai" on BiliBili

Note. The screenshot is from its channel. Source: https://space.BiliBili.com/49637627/

Figure 3.1 displays the homepage of the show on BiliBili, which is one of the most popular videos creating and sharing websites in China. The name "Buk Buk Zaai" (卜卜齋) means the old-style private school (Si Shu 私塾), so this talk show sometimes teaches the usages of Cantonese. However, its target is still the

Cantonese speakers. The most interesting aspect of the show is its mascot, the cartoon ram, as Figure 3.2 shows. According to the producer Buk Zai, the cartoon ram has been designed in 2010 when microblogging (Weibo) was super popular in China. It was created to promote Guangzhou's cultures with social media. Guangzhou's nick name is the City of Rams (Yangcheng 羊城) thus the icon is a speaking and moving ram.

Figure 3.2: The episode "This Canton's Custom Can Help You"

Note. The screenshot is captured from BiliBili. Source: https://reurl.cc/p6GXg8

As depicted in Figure 3.2, the show presents the interactions between the man Buk Lou (卜佬) and the ram. The man represents the older generation whose mother tongue is Cantonese and is familiar with Cantonese. The ram, on the other hand, symbolizes the younger generation, possibly less acquainted with Cantonese. Therefore, the man frequently undertakes the role of an educator or storyteller within the show, while the ram, representing the audience, poses inquiries or acquires knowledge. Despite the show's use of animated storytelling, its viewership extends beyond just children and teenagers. In reality, the audience's age range spans from 20 to 40 years old.

Table 3.1 lists the episodes related to Cantonese and Cantonese people spanning from 2016 to August 2022. As a short video channel, each episode maintains a duration of approximately 5 minutes. Within the compilation of 40 episodes, two main features of Cantonese are highlighted: ancient and mixture. First, the old age of Cantonese is exemplified in the episode "Cantonese's pronunciation makes you feel like watching costume dramas" (see Figure 3.3) that a considerable number of Cantonese expressions preserve the classical Chinese style (Wen Yan Wen 文言文) in vocabulary and grammar. Essentially, speaking Cantonese, in a sense, mirrors the act of speaking in classical Chinese.

Table 3.1: The Selected Episodes on BiliBili from 2016-August 2022

Date	Duration	Title/Theme	Viewed by
2016-11-07	02:19m	the brutal Cantonese people	76K
2017-01-26	03:10m	the history of Cantonese New Year's songs	39K
2017-05-22	02:36m	A foreigner wrote a Cantonese textbook 200 years ago.	25K
2017-06-05	02:47m	Have you felt Cantonese's sound effects with mouth?	213K
2017-06-19	02:55m	We still don't know that day when we saw Cantonese's names	77K
2017-06-28	02:40m	Sun Yat-sen University	31K
2017-07-28	05:06m	the advertisement songs of the 1990s	191K
2017-09-20	03:22m	Cantonese's pronunciation makes you feel like watching costume dramas.	91k
2018-02-15	03:07m	Was Kung Hei Fat Choi made by Cantonese people?	40K
2018-03-30	03:16m	You may need to speak these Cantonese if you travel back to Canton 100 years ago.	60K
2018-10-08	03:55m	the earliest collection of Cantonese children's songs	65K
2018-12-30	03:11m	How was the Cantonese nursery rhyme in 1905?	60K
2019-02-03	02:38m	Cantonese likes to put on Fai Chun (lucky messages).	52K
2019-06-11	05:27m	What did Cantonese people do 100 years ago?	84K
2020-01-23	04:41m	Knowledge about Tung Shing in 5 minutes	77K
2020-02-11	01:15m	Cantonese's daily life during the pandemic	47K
2020-03-02	05:54m	Why Cantonese people feel "Yelang Disco" weird?	549K
2020-03-16	05:58m	Have you heard of the 100-year-old Cantonese riddles?	101K
2020-04-01	06:10m	some slangs of Cantonese's visit of grave on Tomb-sweeping Day	72K
2020-05-08	04:18m	the Cantonese's Enlightenment of Rhythm you don't know	71K
2020-06-30	05:12m	the store names which only Cantonese understands	173K
2020-07-10	05:46m	What is the experience when Cantonese people watch "The Bad Kids"?	256K
2020-08-13	03:16m	the store names which only Cantonese people understands	288K
2020-08-26	01:36m	Cantonese people's life philosophy	91K
2020-10-26	02:37m	the store names which only Cantonese people understands	158K
2021-03-04	01:16m	This Canton's custom can help you.	45K
2021-03-10	03:40m	the store names which only Cantonese people understands IV	109K
2021-04-28	02:42m	the store names which only Cantonese people understands V	147K
2021-05-31	03:43m	Is movie "White Snake" worthy to watch?	64K
2021-07-30	02:41m	the Cantonese's Enlightenment of Rhythm you don't know	45K
2021-08-16	03:56m	the store names which only Cantonese understands VI	138K

Date	Duration	Title/Theme	Viewed by
2021-09-18	04:05m	the most popular dim sum of Yum cha	64K
2021-12-20	03:36m	Do you know the meaning of lion head in lion dance?	74K
2022-03-31	03:03m	This is how Cantonese people argue with each other in childhood.	622K
2022-04-30	02:51m	Have you heard of these weird place names of Guangdong?	239K
2022-05-27	04:16m	What was the experience of writing titles in Cantonese 100 years ago?	43K
2022-07-04	02:14m	the store names which only Cantonese people understands VII	76K
2022-07-20	01:45m	the product names that break Cantonese's values	193K
2022-08-03	02:02m	Have you played these language games in the past?	33K
2022-08-17	02:22m	Did the Sushi restaurant ban employees to speak Cantonese?	230K

Moreover, within the compilation of these 40 episodes, a significant proportion—approximately one third—focuses directly on historical topics. For example, one episode articulates that during the Qing Empire, teaching foreigners Cantonese was not allowed, but Cantonese was eventually recorded into a textbook alongside English and Cantonese Pinyin by the missionaries for foreigners to learn in 1828. One episode shares the spoken and written Cantonese in society 100 years ago. In a similar vein, another episode traces back the collected Cantonese children's songs in 1928, which have affected several generations.

Figure 3.3: The episode "Cantonese Pronunciation Makes You Feel Like Watching Costume Dramas."

Note. The screenshot is captured from BiliBili. Source: https://reurl.cc/AA5Dke

Other episodes, to a certain extent, relate to the sources of the well-known phrases, music, customs, habits, and so on. For example, the most popular and influential Lunar New Year's blessing, "Kung Hei Fat Choy" (wish you prosperous 恭喜發財), was from a Cantonese businessman and documented in a nineteenth-century book by an American businessman. Through these episodes, the producer Buk Zai tries to tell the audience the underlying reasons and rules of Cantonese, which are often taken for granted by its users.

The aforementioned episodes reflect the long history and early internationalization of Cantonese. As the book mentioned before, Guangzhou is famous for its trade role in history, and it has deep connections with foreign businessmen. Therefore, in relation to the second feature, mixture, Cantonese has not only integrated English vocabulary since the nineteenth century but has also been documented in both English and Cantonese Pinyin to disseminate. It should be noted that the Cantonese Pinyin and writing system are not taught at public schools in Guangdong, and parents either lack interest or ability to teach their children Cantonese at home. As a result, many Cantonese native speakers in Guangdong are unfamiliar with Cantonese spelling and writing. Their Cantonese basically acquires from a family speaking environment and Cantonese-speaking dramas, music, and movies. The absence of Cantonese education leads to an uneven development between oral and written Cantonese.

Figure 3.4: The episode "Teach You 9 Sounds & 6 Tones in 3 Minutes"

Note. The screenshot is captured from its BiliBili channel. Source: https://reurl.cc/K0GDAg

When Buk Zai introduced the rule of nine sounds and six tones in the episode (refer to Figure 3.4), numerous Cantonese native speakers commented that they did not hear about or understand what he said, including the historical materials he shared in videos. Aside from the entry-level language knowledge, Buk Zai also introduced the enlightenment training of phonetic rhetoric, such as rhythm rules (Shenglv 聲律) and counting baak laam (Rap 數白欖) even though the viewers are adults. These kinds of knowledge should have been learned completely during childhood, but now they are approached a little on social media. When native speakers lose the learning and speaking environment with the declining Hong Kong's cultural industries and parents' reluctance to learn Cantonese, there is no way to stop Cantonese from waning.

Other Cantonese collections, for example, the episode "This is how Cantonese people argue with each other during childhood." reviewed the popular jingles among children when they fight. There is no clue who created these jingles and why they are popular, but children in primary schools learn them from TV dramas and even from each other. In the era before the internet, the jingles united the whole Cantonese-speaking areas that almost every child had ever heard of or used them. The episode received not only the highest hit rate but also nearly 3000 responses from netizens with their sharing of memories and different versions of certain jingles. Since these jingles are used in fighting, most are rude and offensive but present very strong Cantonese characteristics in rhyme and meaning. The following three examples are some of the most well-known jingles:[1]

(1) "頭 tau 大 daai 無 mou 腦 nou, 腦 nou 大 daai 生 saang 草 cou"
"big head without brain, big brain with growing grasses"

(2) "識 sik 少 siu 少 siu, 扮 baan 代 doi 表 biu"
"[someone] knows a little [of something] but pretends to be an expert"

(3) "癡 ci 癡 ci 呆 ngo 呆 ngo 坐 co 埋 maai 一 jat 臺 toi，戇 ngong 戇 ngong 居 geoi 居 geoi 企 kei 埋 maai 一 jat 堆 deoi"
"the foolish people sit and stand together [to do something boring and stupid]"

However, in accordance with the comments under the episode, these jingles seem to prevail among the Cantonese speakers born in the 1980s-1990s only. These jingles, to a certain group of Cantonese speakers, present not so much the unpleasant experience of fighting as their talents in expression. Fighting with jingles sounds more like a verbal competition. As one viewer commented, "if you don't recite the jingles, you will lose in the fight." When children grow up, they either forget these jingles or have limited opportunities to use them, let alone the generation born after 2000 who has less chance to speak

---

[1] Three sentences can be used to mock or satire a stupid and arrogant person.

Cantonese. Fighting, to the younger generation, becomes speaking dirty words in Mandarin, which makes viewers of the episode feel sad and uncomfortable.

Furthermore, the crisis of Cantonese, which also causes disputes with Mandarin, is highlighted in the show. In the episode "What is the experience when Cantonese speakers watch '*The Bad Kids*' (隱秘的角落),"[2] Buk Zai expressed the current gap in Cantonese language proficiency between parents and children. In the drama, the father spoke Cantonese with his partners but switched to Mandarin when speaking with his son. This marked scene also caused many netizens' strong responses to the episode. They used their life, memories, and sufferings as examples to discuss the status of Cantonese in Guangdong. Two consensuses were reached among the discussions: Mandarin is replacing Cantonese at home and school among the younger generation; the variants of Cantonese beyond Guangzhou should be respected.

In the second most viewed and the most commented episode, "Why Cantonese people feel Yelang Disco weird?", the content led to debates between Cantonese and Mandarin. The popular song "Yelang Disco" is sung in Mandarin but incorporates some Cantonese pronunciations. Thus, the mixture of two unintelligible languages makes the song sound weird. Buk Zai explained that the multiple sounds of Cantonese led to the mismatch in the rhythm of the song. Nevertheless, the topic received many meaningless attacks, such as regional discrimination, language confrontation, and accent privilege. It is apparent that the comments or discussions under the episode deviate from the original intention of the topic. As the book mentioned earlier, the imbalance of development among regions in China and the uniqueness of Cantonese give rise to many cultural contradictions. Some features of Cantonese, especially the distinctive pronunciation, are usually imitated by the actors in Mandarin-speaking dramas, movies, and skits to mock. Hence, as a Cantonese talk show on social media, its audience and influence are limited, and it has to face the ongoing confrontations between Cantonese lovers and haters.

In addition, dialects on censorship have certain advantages on social media. Buk Zai sometimes utilizes the distinctions between Cantonese and Mandarin in meaning and pronunciation to explain the features. These distinctions often lead to ridiculous consequences because some normal expressions in Mandarin can be offensive, embarrassing, or dirty in Cantonese. As a result, some sensitive topics or phrases spoken in Cantonese are permitted, while those spoken in Mandarin can be detected and censored on BiliBili.

However, Buk Zai also suffered other complicated situations. He shared an experience where he made a comparison between the Mandarin and

---

[2] The drama was shot in Zhanjiang where Jyut, Min, and Hakka dialects can be heard.

Cantonese versions of the Japanese animation "Pokémon" in an episode, but he had to delete it soon after due to accusations of secession from viewers. The constant debates between Cantonese speakers and non-Cantonese speakers have necessitated Buk Zai's great caution in setting the agenda of the show. Moreover, certain political contents are restricted by BiliBili. Buk Zai has uploaded a picture of the lyricist Albert Leung in an episode, but the video was removed without any explanations. He assumed that Albert Leung's support for Hong Kong's dissidents caused his pictures and words to be denied. The platforms out of China may help Buk Zai bypass some censorship, but the cost of crossing the Great Firewall forces him to abandon social media such as Facebook, YouTube, and Instagram. In all, the pressure of operations and the risk of censorship on an individual channel are higher.

Crazy Canton

Compared with the individualized talk show "Cantonese Buk Buk Zaai", "Crazy Canton" was operated by a team from different departments which formed stable and high-quality content production. It was created in 2016 without a specific purpose and long-term plan at the beginning and adopted the form of stand-up comedy. Figure 3.5 shows its homepage on BiliBili. The show broadcasted weekly, with each episode lasting over ten minutes and featuring survey and research data. The core and iconic member of the team is the host Guo Jiafeng (see Figure 3.6), who is also the host of TVS in reality.

Figure 3.5: The homepage of the Crazy Canton on BiliBili

Note. The screenshot is captured from its channel. Source: https://space.BiliBili.com/23080377

The show primarily focused on the cultures of Canton and the Cantonese people. Among the 70 episodes, 38 of them served as introductions to common topics or concepts relevant to the local population. While these topics might not be widely known to local Cantonese people, they are likely to have encountered them during their upbringing. Simultaneously, as a general cultural and entertainment show, its audience included both non-Cantonese migrants within Guangdong and individuals who do not speak Cantonese from outside the province. As a result, the show's themes in fact attracted a larger number of non-Cantonese speakers.

Figure 3.6: The Episode 1 of the Crazy Canton

Note. The screenshot is captured from its BiliBili channel.
Source: https://reurl.cc/RzNDb9

Even though the show was not designed to teach Cantonese, for non-Cantonese speakers it also provides the pronunciation and explanations of certain phrases mentioned in videos for reference. Figure 3.7 illustrates one example of one episode with Cantonese Pinyin and meanings. The ram at the left corner of the screen was the mascot of the show "Me Aa" (咩啊), which means "what" in Cantonese.

Figure 3.7: The example of Cantonese's learning time

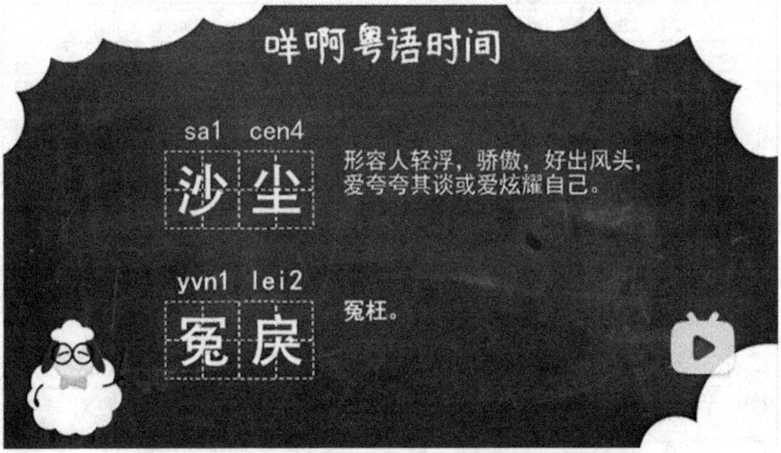

Note. The screenshot is captured from its BiliBili channel.
Source: https://reurl.cc/QXMLpZ

Furthermore, Guo Jiafeng stated his or the team's stance on Cantonese development in the video. In the first episode (see Table 3.2), the title has already conveyed his thoughts on the crisis of Cantonese. In his opinion, as long as people kept speaking Cantonese and making Cantonese shows, Cantonese would not disappear. On the contrary, local people should worry about the fading of "Bao Dong Gua" (煲冬瓜), the Mandarin with a strong Cantonese accent, which means Cantonese speakers can speak standard Mandarin without an accent under the widespread Mandarin education. Thus, he argued that Mandarin helped communication, and Cantonese could continue to evolve by incorporating Mandarin words.

Table 3.2: The selected episodes on BiliBili from 2016-September 2017

Date	Ep	Duration	Theme/Title	Tag	Viewed by
2016-02-06	1	04:57m	Cantonese will be inherited if we continue to speak.	hau kam	80K
2016-03-14	5	11:05m	Why was ATV closed?	ATV	72K
2016-04-08	8	11:09m	the knowledge of mixture of English and Cantonese	4A tone	700K
2016-04-22	10	18:15m	There is one thing that Cantonese people don't dare to eat	food	156K
2016-05-06	12	11:13m	Sun yat-sen and Cantonese Opera	Cantonese Opera	83K
2016-05-13	13	16:19m	the story of Leslie Cheung and Nanhai Shi-san Lang	Cantonese Opera	81K
2016-06-03	16	16:32m	the guidance of Guangdong's colleges	the entrance exam	78K
2016-06-16	17	11:52m	Beyond and me	Beyond	74K
2016-07-03	20	16:30m	I bet you must watch these advertisements.	advertisement	256K
2016-07-10	21	19:43m	the Stand-up comedian Dayo Wong	Dayo Wong	225K
2016-07-16	22	20:11m	the history of TVB	TVB	107K
2016-07-24	23	21:45m	the classic animation	childhood, animation	184K
2016-08-21	27	15:32m	the classic nursery rhymes	childhood, nursery rhymes	75K
2016-08-28	28	12:01m	Canton and Saam Gwok	game	57K
2016-09-10	30	20:35m	Will you think of Lesile Cheung when you see stars?	Leslie Cheung	117K
2016-10-08	33	12:26m	the history of Naam Jyut Gwok	the king of Naam Jyut	60K
2016-10-15	34	21:51m	Bruce Lee	Kung fu	89K
2016-11-12	38	20:24m	Sun yat-sen University	university motto	154K
2016-11-19	39	22:16m	Sam Hui	Cantonese songs	151K
2016-12-03	41	30:23m	the eating and caring habit in Fall and Winter	makeup	73K

Date	Ep	Duration	Theme/Title	Tag	Viewed by
2017-01-07	45	18:30m	This drama has over 3000 episodes	migrant wives, local husbands	168K
2017-01-14	46	22:36m	How to make thirteen orphans?	Canton Mahjong	123K
2017-01-21	47	20:36m	Spring Festival	Year of the Rooster	68K
2017-03-05	48	12:20m	Does Cantonese have cultures?	poems	126K
2017-03-11	49	16:19m	Stephen Chow	comedy movie	73K
2017-03-18	50	13:14m	Where is the source of Canton culture?	Gwong Fu	59K
2017-04-01	52	15:52m	The knowledge of Tomb-Sweeping Day	holiday	58K
2017-04-08	53	15:45m	Cheung Wai Kin	childhood, actor	113K
2017-05-05	57	14:15m	anti-corruption dramas	Hong Kong, ICAC	77K
2017-05-19	59	11:09m	discrimination map	United Airlines	91K
2017-06-10	62	11:18m	Do you know what Bao Dong Gua is?	Cantonese, Mandarin	136K
2017-06-17	63	12:23m	Wayne Lai Yiu Cheung	actor	140K
2017-06-24	64	10:22m	four rules of Yum Cha	Dim sum	417K
2017-08-11	65	10:41m	No Hong Kong, No Current Cantonese	Hong Kong	89K
2017-08-25	67	11:32m	Hong Kong movies	movie	71K
2017-09-02	68	10:18m	Liang Qichao and Cha Chaan Teng	Cha chaan teng	103K
2017-09-08	69	12:08m	Eason Chan	singer	107K
2017-09-15	70	09:19m	Hong Kong's Zombie movies	zombie	162K

Guo Jiafeng is quite optimistic about the future of Cantonese. However, the show's audience, most Cantonese speakers, could not be convinced by typing different comments on screen and under the video. They still believed that the promotion of Mandarin was so strong that fewer and fewer residents could speak Cantonese. Moreover, they also thought that the protection of Cantonese could not rely on Hong Kong alone.

Netizens' comments, in fact, declared Hong Kong's indispensable impact on Cantonese. Although the show mainly introduced Guangdong's cultures by referring to the well-known food, music, colleges, dramas, celebrities, and entertainment in Guangdong, the number of episodes about Hong Kong in Table 3.2 is 19, half of 38 episodes. Even Guo Jiafeng's acting style in the show was affected by two Hong Kong artists, Dayo Wong and Stephen Chow. In the episode "No Hong Kong, No Current Cantonese" (see Figure 3.8), he briefly introduced the modern history of Hong Kong, and his conclusion received the most approvals from the audience on BiliBili and YouTube.

The approvals from the Cantonese speakers in Guangdong, Hong Kong, and Malaysia all agreed that Hong Kong's economy and cultural industries have strongly promoted Cantonese influence from food, dramas, music, movies, advertisements, and animations. Even if Cantonese speakers and non-Cantonese speakers can easily access Hong Kong's cultural products under globalization, two special creations, namely the public service announcements and the translated Japanese animations on TV, differentiate them from each other.

The public service announcements made or funded by the Hong Kong government on TV channels were formally received by the residents of Guangdong at home in the 1990s. Therefore, the people who were born and grew up in the 1980s and 1990s were affected by Hong Kong extremely strongly. The advanced ideas of freedom of speech, environment protection, occupational safety, professional customer service, and even the positive attitude to life showed in the public service announcements not only become Cantonese people's memories but also integrate into their lives. When Guo Jiafeng cited the slogan of the independent anti-corruption agency "ICAC" in the show, the audience responded on the screen and under the video with the plot of the anti-corruption public service announcement or the lines of other irrelevant public service announcements.

Figure 3.8: The episode "No Hong Kong, No Current Cantonese"

Note. The screenshot is captured from YouTube. Source: https://reurl.cc/M8e0ZL

Also, other public service announcements such as stopping family violence, obeying traffic rules, and the parental guidance of TV programs showed how a civil society looks like even though those rules or laws merely applied in Hong Kong. When public service announcements are broadcasted on TV on days and nights for years, they rub off on Cantonese people gradually. For example, in some comments under the videos, the audience realized the value of the classification system of TV programs and movies despite the fact that the system does not exist in mainland China.

In Guangdong, these public service announcements have another meaning as well. Since information and media are controlled and censored by the Guangdong government, not all of Hong Kong's information is permitted to be broadcast. These public service announcements thus are used to cover some sensitive content, for example, political news. When one or several public service announcements appear suddenly in a news program, the people know some contents are being hidden. This scene which was satirized by Guo Jiafeng in the show only occurs in the Guangdong area.

Besides, Japanese animations widened the horizons of Chinese people and built various imaginal worlds. The numerous roles, stories, and lines of classic animations composed memories for many. For most Chinese people, these animations were usually translated and dubbed in Mandarin after they entered China in the 1980s. However, for Cantonese people, the translations and dubbing were done in their mother tongue on Hong Kong's TV channels. In other words, when a Cantonese person and a non-Cantonese person watch the same Japanese animation, they may call different titles and role names due to their respective translations and viewing habits. Therefore, a quick way to determine whether someone is from Guangdong or not is to ask them about the name or the theme song of a particular animation.

In addition, it is worth noting that similar to the show "Cantonese Buk Buk Zaai," the certain content of "Crazy Canton" also caused the debates of the status between Cantonese and Mandarin. In the episode "Does Cantonese have cultures?" Guo Jiafeng first refuted several popular rumors supported by some Cantonese speakers, then reclaimed that Cantonese shows need to be protected rather than the language itself. The debates under the video were about whether Cantonese is a language. Still, these debates did not lead to any conclusions. People's minds cannot be changed easily by one episode or one show. The concerns of Cantonese dying and the attacks on Cantonese people's mother tongue priority continue.

Canton One Two

The practices of the show "Crazy Canton" brought a successful experience for the team to do short videos. After "Crazy Canton" ended in 2017, the original team turned to do a new show, "Canton One Two". Figure 3.9 shows its homepage on BiliBili. Several typical Cantonese phrases, "Kau Kei" (whatever 求其), "Jam Caa" (drinking tea 飲茶), and "Sai Lei" (amazing 犀利) are highlighted.

Compared with the above two cases in this chapter, the team of Canton One Two is bigger and more professional, composed of departments of writer, editor, art, photography, director, and operation. According to the public interview video with Guo Jiafeng online,[3] the show's agendas are sourced from life experience, hot topics online, and locality. Before filming, the agenda is discussed and decided by writers and editors. If editors reach a plateau, playing games helps to solve this problem.

Figure 3.9: The homepage of Canton One Two

Note. The screenshot is captured from its official account on BiliBili.
Source: https://reurl.cc/o7jQv3

Compared with the above two Cantonese talk shows, Canton One Two pays more attention to attracting non-Cantonese speaking audiences by adding more Mandarin and non-Guangdong elements into each episode, although the show's slogan is "creating Cantonese new popularity." To make the show interesting and tempting, in addition to discussing topics such as young people's relationships, jobs, life, and online games, the show also features various performance and interaction methods. These include role-playing, location shooting, food tasting, team competitions, and interviews with celebrities, which appear as main content or in post-credit scenes.

As a Cantonese talk show on mainland China's social media, its success is rare and stunning. It gains ongoing funding from various sponsors, including local businesses, as well as a growing following. Additionally, it has developed into an offline show, with the team holding their first talk show in a theater in March 2018.[4] The team also organizes stand-up comedy competitions and stage shows to discover and train local talents. On the popular short-video platform TikTok, their channel has attracted over 12 million followers.

Table 3.3 lists 129 episodes about Cantonese and Cantonese people that were produced from 2017 to December 2021. Even though the topics are various, 15 episodes are about Guangdong's food. In particular, the episodes about ice

---

[3] The video can be found at https://www.bilibili.com/s/video/BV1D4411z7rt

[4] The report of the talk show can be found at https://read01.com/M27BRg7.html#.ZC3L13bMK00

cream and rice rolls receive more than 10,000 comments each. The episode "The ranking of ice-creams in Cantonese people's heart" touched many Cantonese people by memorizing the ice cream tastes in a child's eyes and the local brand which grew up with the 20-30 years old Cantonese people with an affordable price. As for rice roll (Coeng Fan 腸粉), it has become one of the most famous Dim Sum in and beyond Guangdong and can be found in every Cantonese-style restaurant in and out of China. Under the episode "Rice roll is the best breakfast," the audience from different areas of Guangdong shared their cooking and eating styles of rice rolls actively.

Table 3.3: The selected episodes on BiliBili from 2017-December 2021

Date	Ep	Duration	Theme/title	Tag	Viewed by
2017-04-17	62	02:07 m	Why Cantonese likes to be late so much?	socialization	147K
2017-05-04	79	03:27 m	What is the experience of dating a Cantonese guy?	relationship	108K
2017-05-13	88	04:24 m	How good is Cantonese mother?	Mother's Day, kinship	34K
2017-05-19	94	02:42 m	What is the experience of dating a Cantonese girl?	520, relationship, girl friend	109 K
2017-05-30	105	02:48 m	Why Cantonese likes taking shower so much?	routine life, singing	177K
2017-05-31	106	04:15 m	How Cantonese celebrates the Children's Day?	childhood memory, children's day	185K
2017-06-17	123	03:30 m	How amazing is Cantonese father?	Father's Day, kinship	80K
2017-06-25	131	02:50 m	Cantonese's mess hall at midnight is far more than an instant food	mess hall at midnight	301K
2017-06-29	135	02:47 m	Why Canton's weather is so abnormal?	summer, air conditioner	130K
2017-07-02	138	03:37 m	How scary is Cantonese's cockroach?	southern cockroach	729K
2017-07-15	151	04:06 m	How much does Cantonese like travel?	travel	79K
2017-07-23	159	03:55 m	How much does Cantonese like Cantonese songs?	Cantonese songs, boy friend	399K
2017-07-24	160	03:38 m	How scary is Cantonese's mosquito?	mosquito, summer	199k
2017-08-14	181	03:55 m	How much does Cantonese like to watch TVB?	Hong Kong drama	254K
2017-08-31	198	03:15 m	What folk medicine did your parents let you try?	folk medicine	134K
2017-09-08	206	03:01 m	Have you suffered hurricane?	climate, disaster	169K

Date	Ep	Duration	Theme/title	Tag	Viewed by
2017-10-03	231	03:57 m	How Cantonese celebrates the Mid-Autumn Festival?	lantern, reunion, custom	128K
2017-10-07	235	04:43 m	What Cantonese likes to do when they are in traffic congestion?	traffic congestion, national day	278K
2017-10-15	243	03:31 m	Have you been asked these questions?	Cantonese, rich redneck	508K
2017-10-17	245	03:20 m	Have you drunk herbal tea?	herbal Tea	257K
2017-10-21	249	03:20 m	How elusive is Cantonese's weather?	summer, winter	375K
2017-10-26	254	03:29 m	Your McDonald uncle is online	McDonald's	163K
2017-10-30	258	03:58 m	What will happen when Cantonese visit haunted house?	Halloween, haunted house	253K
2017-11-03	262	04:00 m	You are not standard Cantonese if you don't eat crab in Fall	seaside, seafood	125K
2017-12-08	297	04:04 m	What does Cantonese eat in Winter?	winter, Southerners	104K
2017-12-13	302	02:51m	Do you remember how many classic TVB advertisements?	classic, Hong Kong	237K
2017-12-22	310	05:42 m	How does Cantonese keep warm in Winter?	winter, keep warm	195K
2018-01-11	331	04:19 m	How Cantonese develops eating hotpot to martial art?	hot pot	202K
2018-01-24	344	03:28 m	You must hear Cantonese's several popular nick names.	friends, nick names	241K
2018-01-30	350	05:57 m	Why cannot Cantonese make a New Year's visit on the third day of new year?	Chinese New Year, custom	136K
2018-02-08	359	04:08 m	How much will Cantonese give gift cash on wedding?	wedding, gift cash	194K
2018-02-13	363	04:27 m	What if we don't receive red packets during the Chinese New Year?	red packets	231K
2018-02-15	367	02:57 m	The New Year's songs for Cantonese	new year's songs	111k
2018-03-02	381	07:11 m	What is the difference between Cantonese's and Northeast's lai see?	lai see	319K
2018-03-17	396	04:09m	Cantonese's snacks	memory, snacks	336K
2018-04-01	411	03:42m	Why we miss Lesile Chuang every year?	Lesile Chuang	169K
2018-04-07	417	03:28m	Wui Naam Tin decides everything.	continuous warm and wet weather	258K

The Image of Cantonese People 31

Date	Ep	Duration	Theme/title	Tag	Viewed by
2018-04-08	418	03:33m	You cannot have a romantic relationship with someone by imitating the stories of Hong Kong dramas.	relationship	190K
2018-04-15	425	03:40m	Why Cantonese people like to watch TVB's dramas when eating meals?	Hong Kong drama	217K
2018-05-16	456	03:41m	What is the embarrassing moment to Cantonese speakers?	attention seekers	391K
2018-05-18	458	04:16m	How long you have not barbecued?	BBQ, Summer	259K
2018-05-25	465	04:23m	You are familiar with the scene by watching Hong Kong movies.	rascals	60K
2018-05-26	466	07:08m	We redefine Cantonese's acceptance of tasting spicy hot pot.	Sichuan hot pot	360K
2018-06-01	472	07:50m	My wish of Children's Day is to play in amusement arcade.	amusement arcade	94K
2018-06-14	485	04:36m	The flooding life in Guangdong after heavy rain	flood	342K
2018-06-16	486	04:51m	Is it true that Guangdong has many rich people?	rich people	218K
2018-07-22	523	04:21m	Which kind of tong sui do you like?	sweet soup	552K
2018-08-21	553	04:55m	The ranking of ice creams in Cantonese's heart	ice cream, memory	601K
2018-09-16	579	03:25m	How Cantonese people views Typhoon Shanzhu?	typhoon	381K
2018-09-18	581	03:14m	How to prove you are Cantonese?	dishes cleaning	445K
2018-09-25	588	03:37m	The Cantonese's legendary creature in office environment	legendary creature	148K
2018-10-24	617	03:24m	The Cantonese's spirit in Autumn is to eat, sleep well and keep hope.	upset of Autumn	127K
2018-10-29	622	04:01m	Cantonese's travel habit is formed at primary school.	Autumn travel	105K
2018-10-31	623	05:56m	The shadow of eating fish	fish	309K
2018-11-08	631	04:05m	The watchwords of Cha chaan teng	Hong Kong-style cafés	606K
2018-12-01	654	04:59m	How amazing is Guangzhou?	Guangzhou, ranking	315K
2018-12-06	659	09:29m	My youth starts from Eason Chan.	Eason Chan, album	267K
2018-12-23	676	05:05m	Do you know why Winter Solstice is more important than the new year?	Winter Solstice	143K
2019-01-13	698	04:29m	Cantonese people's good fortune	Ji Tau	222K

Date	Ep	Duration	Theme/title	Tag	Viewed by
2019-01-17	702	03:42m	Guangdong's unpredictable weather	weather	243K
2019-01-23	707	03:57m	The military training in Winter	military training	128K
2019-02-04	720	03:30m	Are you sure you are Cantonese if you don't stroll around the flower fair?	flower fair	201K
2019-02-04	721	03:30m	You never hear these new version New Year songs.	new year songs	186K
2019-02-16	728	03:25m	Mosquitoes exist in all seasons in Guangdong.	Winter, mosquitoes	197K
2019-02-19	731	09:59m	Opening red packets on the Lantern Festival	lai see	187K
2019-02-22	734	03:32m	Cantonese's caly pot rice in Winter	clay pot rice	301K
2019-02-26	738	03:37m	The most successful TV advertisements must be the animated cartoon.	toy, advertisement	192K
2019-03-27	767	04:54m	Do you know how economical Cantonese is?	save money	253K
2019-04-17	788	03:57m	Why Cantonese likes to eat at Dai Pai Dong?	cooked-food stall	399K
2019-04-25	796	04:26m	The speedy lifestyle in Guangzhou	lifestyle	170K
2019-05-01	802	04:59m	What do Cantonese usually do on holiday?	May day, Mahjong, Karaoke	280K
2019-05-08	809	03:34m	Teaching Mahjong is Cantonese's the tenderest moment.	Mahjong	220K
2019-05-22	823	05:21m	Snowing is Cantonese's the most expected thing all the year round.	snow	166K
2019-05-24	825	04:11m	Rice roll is the best breakfast.	rice roll	1141K
2019-05-27	828	03:11m	We miss second eldest brother forever.	migrant wives, local husbands	703K
2019-06-07	839	05:04m	We Cantonese eat sweet and salty rice dumplings.	Dragon Boat Festival	166K
2019-07-20	882	03:27m	My plain broth is missing.	Double-Flavor Pot	277K
2019-07-21	883	03:59m	Guidance for Cantonese to eat spicy food	spice	528K
2019-07-26	888	03:04m	Body heat is everywhere in Guangdong.	heaty food	253K
2019-08-02	895	04:16m	It is time to prove you are Cantonese for "Ji Jing Bou Jing."	heal an organ by eating the corresponding organ of an animal	172K
2019-08-14	907	04:41m	How Cantonese likes to sing Cantonese songs?	advertisement	433K

The Image of Cantonese People

Date	Ep	Duration	Theme/title	Tag	Viewed by
2019-08-26	918	04:46m	You can see how low-profile Cantonese is when they wear flip flops.	flip-flop	786K
2019-09-08	932	06:01m	You must try Yum Cha in Guangdong.	dim sum, gathering	334K
2019-09-30	954	04:17m	Cantonese determines Ji Tau's explanation.	Ji Tau	210K
2019-10-14	968	02:55m	Wearing shorts Cantonese's way to respect cold front.	cold front	325K
2019-10-22	976	04:20m	Let me tell you how fun to visit Guangdong.	tourism	242K
2019-11-13	998	02:46m	the imagination in Guangdong with heat supply	Winter, heat	279K
2019-11-18	1003	02:15m	Only Cantonese people wear shorts in Winter.	Winter, outfit	174K
2019-11-26	1011	03:28m	Do Cantonese people wear two pairs of pants in Winter?	long underwear	157K
2019-12-22	1036	05:19m	The embarrassing moment to Cantonese people studying outside Canton is to speak Mandarin.	study outside	843K
2019-12-26	1041	04:31m	Teochew people love to drink tea.	Teochew	403K
2020-01-12	1058	02:35m	the first cold front in 2020	cool down	231K
2020-02-17	1090	03:13m	Only Cantonese people can make dozens of dishes with one chicken.	chicken	439K
2020-02-29	1102	03:52m	It is not surprised to wear shorts in February.	warming-up	243K
2020-03-01	1103	04:50m	Swatting at mosquitos at midnight is Cantonese people's first day of March.	mosquito	272K
2020-03-14	1116	04:13m	The fear from continuous warm and wet weather	wui naam tin	227K
2020-03-20	1122	05:36m	Have you collected these toys during childhood?	collection	158K
2020-03-21	1123	04:10m	How amazing is making soup?	soup	324K
2020-03-31	1133	04:00m	Parents' Cantonese Mandarin		860K
2020-04-01	1134	03:29m	Winter comes to Guangdong in April.	weather	265K
2020-04-08	1140	04:29m	the fear from mosquitos at night	mosquito	156K
2020-05-07	1169	04:42m	Cantonese people keep adjusting water temperatures during the bath in Summer.	take hot shower	214K
2020-05-13	1176	02:58m	Cantonese people like rice.	rice	413K
2020-05-15	1177	04:07m	the picnic scene in Guangdong	outdoor picnic	163K
2020-05-22	1184	04:23m	Only Cantonese people roasts thunder amid the torrential rain.	thunder, torrential rain	432K

Date	Ep	Duration	Theme/title	Tag	Viewed by
2020-05-25	1187	03:44m	Why northerner argues Cantonese people are thin?		581K
2020-05-26	1188	03:16m	flying ants after torrential rain	flying ant	316K
2020-06-04	1197	05:21m	Don't call Cantonese people's full name.	etiquette	440K
2020-06-10	1203	04:52m	the suffering under torrential rain	torrential rain	422K
2020-07-03	1226	04:58m	Cantonese people's memory in Bing Sutt	bing sutt	284K
2020-07-06	1229	04:06m	You don't know how good Canton's wet market is.	wet market	540K
2020-08-05	1259	03:50m	What to worry on typhoon day?	typhoon	379K
2020-08-19	1272	03:56m	The basketball team is our pride.	basketball team	169K
2020-09-12	1297	05:12m	What to notice when studying in Guangdong?	weather	227K
2020-10-05	1319	10:26m	the weird place names in Guangdong	competition	422K
2020-10-09	1323	03:53m	the quick switch between warming-up and cooling down	weather	205K
2020-11-12	1341	05:05m	How to make friends in Guangdong?	socializing	204K
2020-11-28	1349	05:17m	Cantonese people cannot sleep well in the cold front.	cool down	335K
2020-12-03	1351	05:20m	the fragile relationships among Cantonese people in Winter	Winter	427K
2021-01-24	1373	04:28m	the struggling with water heater in Winter	water heater	339K
2021-02-01	1374	05:32m	How crazy are Cantonese people about TVB's costume dramas?	costume drama	290K
2021-03-25	1388	04:20m	switching Summer to Winter in one week	weather	277K
2021-04-29	1398	05:13m	the unpredictable rainy day	Rainy day	304K
2021-04-30	1399	02:39m	It is very hard to fall asleep early in Guangdong.	sleeplessness	607K
2021-05-08	1402	03:52m	Holiday is more pathetic than working days.	May Day	251K
2021-05-12	1405	02:49m	Guangzhou metro never loses in the number of passengers.	the metro line 3	829K
2021-07-07	1414	04:32m	How clam Guangzhouer is to the pandemic!	pandemic	552K
2021-12-17	1431	03:34m	the embarrassing moment at the wedding reception	wedding	785K
2021-12-24	-	03:10m	How did Cantonese people spend the eve of New Year from the past to present?	the eve of new year	839K

Also, there are at least 22 episodes about Guangdong's weather in four seasons, and this topic continues to be covered in the episodes produced after 2021. It is the characteristic weather that influences Cantonese people's outfits, diets, eating habits, and ways of thinking. The changing temperatures in one week or even within one day are often complained by the residents, let alone the common sufferings caused by rainstorms and hurricanes. Thus, weather, especially heavy rain and typhoons, ties the people in this area with similar feelings and reflections. Correspondingly, insects, such as cockroaches and mosquitoes under the humid and hot weather, also become the show's hot topics. Struggling with cockroaches or mosquitos in Summer and Winter is a normal part of Cantonese people's lives.

After watching the above episodes, a general image of Cantonese people is constructed. A Cantonese mother is typically skilled in cooking Cantonese dishes, especially soups that are boiled for several hours with various ingredients. When the entire family eats together, they often watch Hong Kong's TV shows, such as news programs or dramas, either during the afternoon or evening. If a Cantonese wants to dine out, the choices are multiple, including food stalls (Dai Pai Dong 大排檔), tea houses (Cha Lao 茶樓), bing sutt (冰室) and cha chaan teng (茶餐廳). Several dishes, such as rice rolls, tong seoi, and clay pot rice are the most popular on the menu. Few Cantonese people eat spicy food, but their bodies often generate heat (Jit Hei 熱氣) due to the hot and humid weather or consumption of fried foods. As a result, mothers of Cantonese people often urge their children to drink herbal tea (涼茶). Cantonese people believe that body heat is the cause of many symptoms, while herbal tea can solve the problems. During holidays, Cantonese people love to travel, play Mahjong, and sing Cantonese songs in karaoke bars with friends. Both classic and new Cantonese songs are mainly from Hong Kong singers. Additionally, nicknames play an essential role in Cantonese people's friendships. People prefer to call each other by nicknames, which usually come from Cantonese dramas or movies, or match their personalities rather than their legal names to show their connection. Regardless of what nicknames mean, they are pronounced very smoothly in Cantonese. These nicknames are created by combining body features, job positions, rankings, English words, and other elements to form unique and distinctive identifiers. For example, Aa Zan (阿珍) as a common name for a girl and Aa Koeng (阿強) as a common name for a boy in the Cantonese-speaking areas become nicknames "Saau Ngaa Zan" (Buck Teeth Zan 哨牙珍) and "Daai Hau Koeng" (Big Mouth Koeng 大口強).

Also, Cantonese people overall are low-profile and down-to-earth. They often dress casually in flip-flops on the streets, regardless of their social status. Guangdong is usually viewed as a rich place, but Cantonese people are pragmatic in their consumption habits. They would rather spend money on things of more value. The most well-known example is the red packets of the

Lunar New Year which has been made fun of many times in the show. In Cantonese eyes, the red packet (紅包/利是) and the gift cash (人情) for a wedding stand as a blessing and not for keeping up with the Joneses. Therefore, 5-10 bucks is a decent amount for a blessing.

Speaking of blessings on joyous occasions, it also brings up Cantonese people's Ji Tau (意頭) principle. Ji Tau is a self-naming behavior to pursue good fortune. Cantonese people try to avoid any negative or unfortunate things by giving good names to stuff like vegetables, animals' organs, numbers, and street/road names, and even creating some tenets to follow on important occasions. Those names usually have nothing to do with the original definitions or the physical features of the objects, but they can make people happy when speaking in Cantonese with positive and pleasing words. People believe that speaking good things a lot will make wishes come true in the end. Compared with the long-lived names/calls, some tenets have been challenged by scientific evidence or have lost their meaning in modern society. Nevertheless, Cantonese people still can interpret in their own way to maintain hope and optimism, as demonstrated in the episode "Cantonese people determines Ji Tau's explanation". If something bad happens, for example, a shattered glass on the ground, Cantonese speakers will say "Lok Dei Hoi Faa, Fu Gwai Wing Waa" (broken things are like blooming flowers to symbolize wealth, honor, and splendor 落地開花 富貴榮華) immediately to pacify emotion. Bad things can be transformed into good things if Cantonese people think from a different perspective.

Apart from the characteristics mentioned above, the image of Cantonese people is distinguished when they are outside of Guangdong. As Figure 3.10 shows in the episode "Studying Outside Guangdong," the straightforward way to identify the Guangdong origin is to speak Cantonese. Two guys in the video sang the theme song of the local sitcom "*Migrant Wives, Local Husbands*" [5] by chance in a public place and called each other "Leng Zai" (handsome guy 靚仔). Then they knew they were from the same place.

---

[5] The drama "Migrant Wives, Local Husband" is made by the Guangdong Radio and Television station and tells the stories of the Kang family and its relatives, friends, neighbors, and workmates in Guangzhou. The story begins with the cross-province and cross-nationality marriages, so multiple languages can be heard in each episode.

Figure 3.10: The episode "Studying Outside Guangdong"

Note. The screenshot is captured from its YouTube channel.
Source: https://reurl.cc/YexXnL

It is understandable that the episode added the element of the sitcom because it cannot be ignored if someone has ever lived in Guangdong. The ongoing sitcom has accompanied several generations since it started to broadcast on TV in 2000 each weekend with more than 4200 episodes. It is a part of the memories of Lou Gwong (Guangzhouer 老廣) as well as opens the door for the non-Cantonese speaking migrants to learn Cantonese. Meanwhile, the iconic call Leng Zai (handsome guy 靚仔) or Leng Neoi (good-looking lady 靚女) used between strangers may not imply a judgment on physical appearance, but it is a more Cantonese style to build a nice, polite, and close relationship. With its widespread usage, it is almost the most recognizable greeting form in a Cantonese context. Considering the existence of Hakka and Teochew dialects in Guangdong, it can be discussed whether speaking Cantonese, especially with the Guangzhou accent, is enough to form the Cantonese people's identity, but the episode, in fact, reflects the mainstream status of Cantonese and its powerful linkage among the residents.

Among the episodes, two used the Chinese word "prove" (證明) in their titles to directly state their proofs as a Cantonese. The first one, "Ji Jing Bou Jing" (以形補形), is shown in Figure 3.11. The phrase in Cantonese is a popular idea of dieting that every Cantonese speaker must hear. It means if you want to keep your organs or parts of your body healthy, you can eat the corresponding organs or a part of an animal or something similar in shape. For example, eating fish benefits the eyes. Figure 3.11 shows a common mother's look who encouraged her children to eat the food she made with the saying Ji Jing Bou

Jing. The scientific evidence supporting the saying is vague and doubtful, but the phrase bonds with mother's love along with a Cantonese's growth.

Figure 3.11: The episode "It is Time to Prove You are Cantonese for 'Ji Jing Bou Jing.'"

Note. The screenshot is captured from its YouTube channel.
Source: https://www.youtube.com/watch?v=4vMKGPoHMgA

The other episode about cleaning dishes highlighted a distinctive aspect of Cantonese people. The habit of cleaning dishes with hot water before eating probably only exists in the Guangdong area. The episode was presented in a slightly exaggerated manner, with a piece of martial arts music accompanying the visuals. As Figure 3.12 shows, after the tea was poured into a cup, two persons pretended to battle with the tea to clean chopsticks, spoons, teacups, and bowls. To Cantonese people, the tea is never for drinking. This dish-cleaning process is called "Long Wun" (啷碗) and consists of a series of steps in order regardless of whether the dishes have been sanitized by the restaurant or not. Most bullet-screen comments from the Cantonese viewers agreed Guo Jiafeng's opinions on Long Wun. "Over real" (過於真實) is the most comment. The reviews under the video were varied by explaining the behavior, sharing the same experience in Guangdong and the embarrassing moments in other places where Long Wun does not exist.

Figure 3.12: The episode "How to Prove You Are Cantonese?"

Note. The screenshot is captured from BiliBili. Source: https://reurl.cc/mDg311

In fact, the video also added two details to assist in identifying Cantonese people. When dining at a restaurant, Cantonese people are provided with a full set of tableware that includes one big bowl, one small bowl, one bone dish, a pair of chopsticks, one spoon, one bowl for soup, one bowl for rice, one teacup, and one glass on the table. A dish of fried vegetables, especially those with green leaves, is a must in every meal as well.

Given the above, it is not hard to find the unique and impressive image of Cantonese people in all aspects of life. Guangdong's environment and weather provide so many food options that its residents develop multiple cooking methods and materials. From seafood and dim sum to fruits, Cantonese people value food and cuisine a lot. Cantonese cuisine is not only one of the four major cuisines in China but also extends to every Chinatown in the world. Aside from pursuing gourmet dishes, Cantonese people also develop the functions of food in "Ji Tau" and "Ji Jing Bou Jing." By giving good names and looking for the valuable parts of food, Cantonese people try to keep an optimistic and healthy mood. The process of "Long Wun" has already become a ritual of life to show people's care and attention.

However, to the show itself, the pressure of daily updates affects the production quality. The recurrent topics, similar copies, and overcentralized contents are often complained about by its fans after the show runs for a few years. Cantonese as a language and culture provides continuous resources for creation, but when the most reachable and noticeable characteristics are disclosed, the team faces the challenge of exploring new resources. Thus, the team decided to adjust the daily status to irregular updates in 2020, which were supported by its fans because they expected high-level content as good as the show "Crazy Canton." Therefore, as Table 3.3 shows, the frequency of the episodes about Cantonese and Cantonese people has decreased since 2021. From May to December 2021, its BiliBili channel published more and more TikTok-style videos to present Cantonese people's characteristics.

Figure 3.13 : The episode "the Embarrassing Moment at the Wedding Reception"

Note. The screenshot is captured from BiliBili. Source: https://reurl.cc/RzNDng

New practices or changes appear in recent episodes. Even though the traditional style, a talking host in front of the camera, usually lasting 4-5 minutes in one episode, is still maintained on BiliBili, it is being replaced with other performing forms. For instance, the online game mode, as shown in Figure 3.13, is added to depict the interactions with a relative in a back-and-forth style during a wedding.

More and more acting scenes are included in recent episodes as well. Sometimes, one episode is composed of several stories without the role of a host. Figure 3.14 shows one of the acting stories which were performed by the team members. Various stories happen at home, in an office environment, in a restaurant, and even in an imagined world. The themes are expressed through the actors' lines and the plots. For example, in the episode "When Guangdong cockroach meets Guangdong flying ant," Cantonese people's life after rainy days was indicated by imagining a blind date between a female cockroach and a male flying ant. According to the episode content and the comments under the episode, viewers out of the Guangdong area can understand why Cantonese people are upset about mosquitoes, cockroaches, and flying ants.

Figure 3.14: The episode "When Guangdong Cockroach Meets Guangdong Flying Ant"

Note. The screenshot is captured from its BiliBili channel.
Source: https://reurl.cc/kX6vNx

The other noticeable change in the show is making shorter videos on TikTok. Videos are shot in portrait mode, which fits mobile phones, and their duration is usually from 15 seconds to one minute, decided by the features of the platform. As a response, the acting or story-telling way becomes the primary form on the show's TikTok channel. To spread the contents widely, these stories are usually dramatic and full of conflicts in plots and dialogues by overplaying Cantonese people's characteristics or the distinctions between Cantonese people and the people from North China (Beifangren 北方人). As Figure 3.15 shows, Guo Jiafeng played the roles of a Cantonese and a northerner. By comparing the amount of money in red packets given in Guangdong and the North, Cantonese people's pragmatism was highlighted even though the term "north" is vague and over-generalized. Such comparisons between Guangdong and the North can be found in many episodes.

Figure 3.15: The episode on Tik Tok

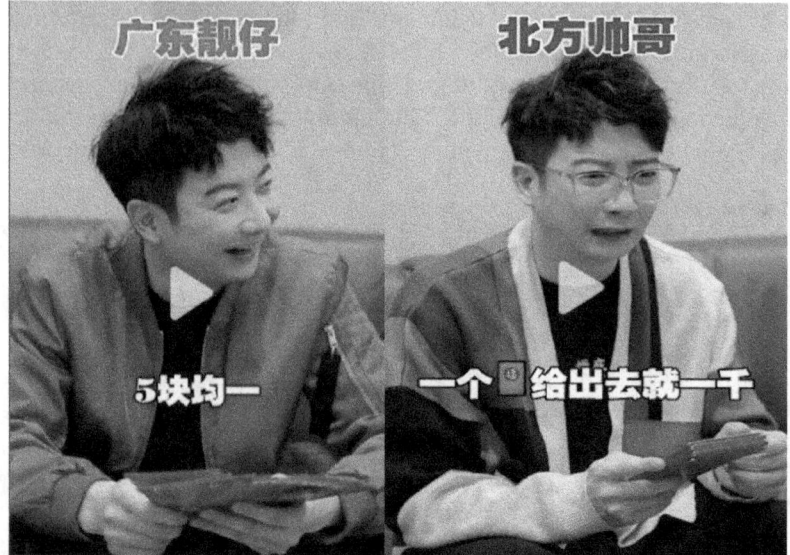

Note. The merged screenshot is captured from its TikTok channel. Source: https://reurl.cc/ZWmMna

Meanwhile, the videos on TikTok seem to cater to the Mandarin speaking viewers more by frequently using Mandarin, even within each episode. Cantonese serves as a role language to stand for Cantonese people or be applied on special occasions. Comparing the videos on BiliBili and TikTok, the former ones are mainly for Cantonese speakers, while the latter ones are for Mandarin speakers or non-Cantonese people. For Cantonese people, the show on BiliBili reminds them of the fragile memories with parents, relatives, and friends as well as their living experience in the Guangdong area with highly summarized and simplified contents. Since the production team and viewers have a common background, there are few barriers to understanding. Therefore, the traditional performing way, oral expression in Cantonese, is not a problem for Cantonese viewers.

For the non-Cantonese viewers, the show on TikTok chooses details to present Guangdong's cultures. There is no host to introduce or explain each characteristic, but viewers can get the point from stories and scenes. Stories often start from puzzles or mistakes and end with surprises. For example, in the episode "When you open a Cantonese's box," a northerner saw the cookie tin and egg roll tin under the tea table at his Cantonese friend's home, only to find that they contained a sewing kit and keys. Using empty biscuit tin as a storage box for the necessary items is a habit of Cantonese people in their homes.

Through the daily interactions between Cantonese and non-Cantonese people, a picture of a Cantonese is gradually constructed.

The show on TikTok also takes the non-Guangzhou elements into account to present Guangdong. The cities or dialects beyond Guangzhou or the Pearl River Delta area become more visible in videos. Under the episode title "How to Integrate into Guangdong Quickly" (see Figure 3.16), five areas were chosen as examples. Instead of describing these places directly, the one-minute episode chose one specific aspect of life in each area. By doing what was shown in the episode, an out-of-towner would integrate into Guangdong.

In Shenzhen (深圳), one guy was working late at night with two big dark circles and said, "coming [to Shenzhen] is the way to integrate." The scene cited one of the most famous slogans, "If you come over, you're a Shenzhener" (來了就是深圳人), to present that Shenzhen as a migrant city welcomes everyone, and people there work super hard to survive. In Chaoshan (潮汕), one guy was inviting viewers to drink tea because tea is essential in local people's lives. In Guangzhou, the scene occurred at the busiest subway Line 3, where office workers used one hand to hold their cell phones and the other hand to hold the hanging strap during one hour commutes. The posture the guy made in the video was imitating kung fu. In Foshan (佛山), the behavior of locking cars responded to the popular phenomenon: residents lock non-residents' vehicles with or without reasons for money. Hence, the guy in the video locked his own car to protect himself. For the last city, Dongguan (東莞), a guy was driving through the Humen bridge that connects the main high-speed ways in Guangdong, and he argued that numerous Cantonese people from different parts of Guangdong could be seen on the bridge. Therefore, to integrate is as easy as to pass the bridge.

Compared with the videos about Cantonese's image on BiliBili, the videos on TikTok generalize Cantonese's characteristics from another perspective. They highlight the signs of the living environment rather than emphasizing the language, diet, and values of Cantonese people. Through years of living under the same weather, temperature, and geographical conditions, newcomers will adopt the behaviors of the inhabitants of Guangdong. In other words, Cantonese people, no matter where they were born, must exhibit similarities in a way.

However, the limitation of the show is evident. Its contents or themes mainly concentrate on the Pearl River Delta area, especially the capital city of Guangzhou, although the name "Canton One Two" refers to the whole Guangdong area, where it gathers multiple dialects/languages, ethnic groups, and customs. Therefore, the show is often complained about by viewers from other parts of Guangdong for ignoring the non-Pearl River Delta area's cultures, customs, and languages.

Figure 3.16: The episode "How to Integrate into Guangdong Quickly?"

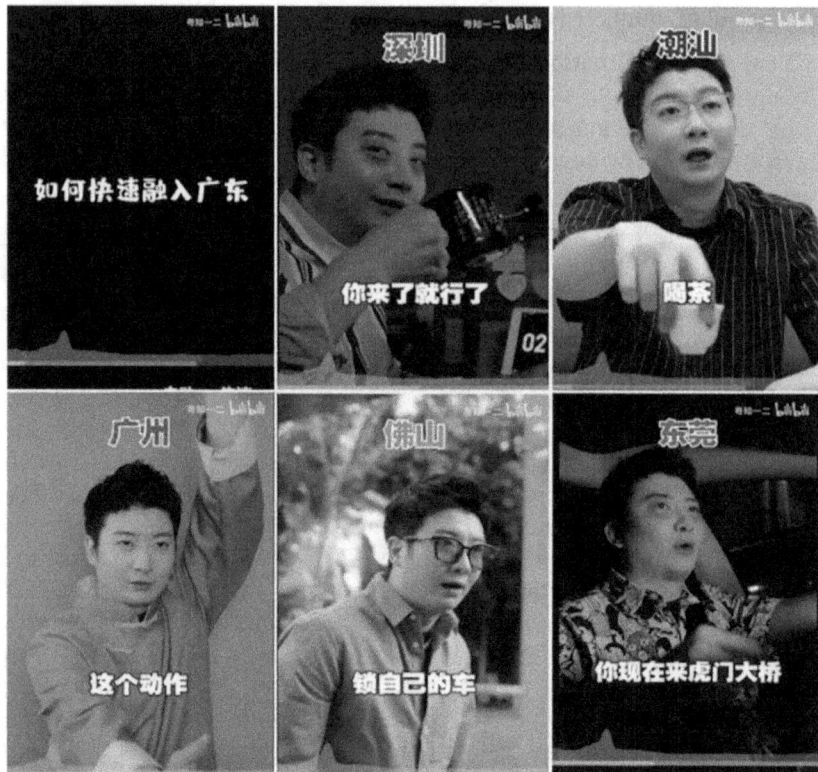

Note. The merged screenshot is captured from its TikTok channel.
Source: https://reurl.cc/94lyZV

In addition, censorship and self-censorship are unspoken agreements between the team and the viewers of BiliBili. This is not just because the rules and terms have been outlined by the platform[6], even though the line between violation and freedom of expression is often ambiguous in China. Aside from the social media within China, the show is also updated on Facebook, YouTube, and Instagram. But the YouTube channel emphasizes "no politics" three times in the description. To the team, none of the topics are related to politics, while Guo Jiafeng or the team often speaks highly of Guangzhou and defends or promotes its policies in the show. During the pandemic, the show encouraged residents to obey the Covid testing policy and the lockdown measures without doubts. Guo Jiafeng sometimes intentionally expresses the risk of sensitive topics in

---

[6] The rules and terms of Bilibili can be found at https://www.bilibili.com/blackboard/topic/activity-cn8bxPLzz.html

episodes to amuse viewers, but the team and the viewers, in fact, understand the risk is not a joke. "Don't let my channel get blocked," a line from Guo Jiafeng toward viewers' mentioning of sensitive topics or words in one episode is serious.

Nevertheless, Guo Jiafeng's attitude to censorship is worthy of rumination. For example, netizens call him Wufeng (污峰), which means "Dirty Guo Jiafeng" as he often says dirty words in Cantonese, which are bleeped in the show, and talks about sex indirectly. Dirty words are forbidden by the platform, and sex topics are not encouraged, but he seems not to worry about mentioning them.

Given the above, the three talk shows present different styles and purposes. "Cantonese Buk Buk Zaai" and "Crazy Canton" are mainly for Cantonese speakers and inhabitants. The former show focuses more on the language with history and knowledge, which also reflects Cantonese people's views, while the latter show reminds Hong Kong's deep impacts on Cantonese and the residents. "Canton One Two" caters to both Cantonese and non-Cantonese speakers and strives to explore different facets of Cantonese cultures with imagination and creativity. It is important to note that the Cantonese language was not the foremost motivation for producers to do shows at the beginning, but they all felt the power of the internet and social media in China around 2014-2016. The more accessible technology and the far-reaching social platforms support many people's ideas. At this point, Cantonese is more like a resource for creating. For example, Buk Zai, who was working at a TV station, decided to turn to new media, namely Weibo and WeChat. On his trip to new media, he felt a sense of responsibility towards his mother tongue. Viewers' feedback and the popularity of Mandarin among local teenagers motivated him to continue the show.

In summary of the above three shows, from the perspective of contents and topics, at least three facets are worthy of discussion. The first facet is the represented and performed Cantonese and Guangdong people's image. Three shows construct a general Cantonese image from four perspectives: Cantonese as the essential symbol of learning from family and Cantonese-speaking dramas, movies, and music; eating or making Cantonese cuisine in certain ways; the huge gaps with other parts of China from diet to the thinking way; and the influences of Hong Kong cultures and civilization. After watching their episodes, it is very easy to distinguish Cantonese people from Chinese people with their abundant characteristics in language and lifestyle. The analyzed online shows have displayed how Cantonese and Guangdong cultures as resources support the local young people's ongoing creation. To survive in the highly competitive environment of short video making, their imagination, ideas, and innovation are expected. In particular, "Canton One Two" keeps trying new forms and various presenting ways on different platforms, while

"Cantonese Buk Buk Zaai" reaches multiple Cantonese topics from history to trendy events under limited conditions. Nevertheless, these ongoing shows face the same challenge of generating innovative and insightful content. After repeating the topics of weather, cuisine, and habits a hundred times, it is important and meaningful to refresh and enrich the image of Cantonese people beyond stereotypes by exploring more unknown fields. For example, the show "Crazy Canton" has introduced the history of Naam Jyut Gwok (Nanyue empire 南越國) while other similar practices related to Cantonese people, such as The Lanfang Republic[7] (蘭芳共和國) and the pirate groups during the Ming and Qing dynasties have not been explored by Cantonese channels so far.

The second facet is the creators' attitude to Cantonese development. Guo Jiafeng or his team is optimistic about Cantonese, and he advocates supporting Cantonese creation, not language. While facing the shrinking Cantonese-speaking population, Buk Zai remains cautiously optimistic because he thinks there is space for Cantonese to exist. However, based on viewers' reactions under channels, creators' optimism cannot relieve the concerns of Cantonese. In comparison to the early reopening period, the popularity of Cantonese in mainland China has waned a lot. Less and less words or phrases sourced from Cantonese are being used or acknowledged by the non-Cantonese speakers. Mandarin, conversely, is affecting Cantonese by penetrating its tones and phrases. To date, Cantonese is more like a symbol of the past, a connection to Hong Kong, or an emotion of reminiscence. Overall, it means something old and gone, just like the aging generation who has ever worshiped Hong Kong's entertainment industry. Accordingly, a more pressing question lying in front of all Cantonese promoters is how to make Cantonese fashionable again. When the influence of Hong Kong's entertainment industry weakens, it is time for Guangdong's creators to chart a new course in the local and overseas markets.

Besides, Cantonese and Guangdong cultures are vast topics with a long history and a variety of facets. Even though it is unlikely to refer to everything of Guangdong, it is important not to overlook the other two subgroups, namely Teochew and Hakka people, who also reside in the same region. In the growing experience of an ordinary Cantonese, the mother tongue education in a public system is absent, not to mention the connection to other subgroups' cultures. Under the strong Cantonese or Gwong Fu (廣府) culture influence, Cantonese speakers know little about non-Cantonese speaking areas. That is why there are disputes about a standard accent among Cantonese people. On a positive note,

---

[7] The Lanfang Republic was a regime founded by Luo Fangbo in the Kalimantan Island from 1777-1884. Luo Fangbo is also viewed as the first Chinese president in the world.

the TV show and three talk shows mentioned above on social media, in fact, open doors for Cantonese people to know about their languages and themselves.

And the third facet is the censorship and self-censorship in the Chinese internet. Censorship from platforms and administration is always a severe and long-term hindrance to online content generation. Among three cases, the platforms within China form a set of rules and terms for users and content with ambiguous standards. The shadow of censorship also extends to the non China platforms where they build channels for global Cantonese speakers. Compared with Mandarin in China, dialect barriers probably make more space to express, for example, dirty words in dialects on social media, but the space can be shrunk randomly. The language barrier is never a hindrance to censorship when it comes to political topics, let alone self-censorship, which can climb over the Great Firewall. Hence, these shows are unable to openly criticize local and central governments and their policies.

Another significant problem related to the censorship of these creators is the huge gaps in economy, cultures, development levels, and ideas between Guangdong and other provinces. Since Guangdong is viewed as a wealthy and advanced region in China, using Cantonese in some people's eyes is one of the ways to assert superiority. If these gaps cannot be removed, the attacks and defamation of Cantonese will not stop. Protecting Cantonese online can be accused of advocating independence or secession even though the liaison between both is reluctant. There is no doubt that such meaningless disputes and accusations only constrain the development of Cantonese creation in China.

Chapter 4

Civil Practices for Cantonese Prospect

Language is not a means of passive reflection of reality but a form of action being used by human being to affect or change the world they speak about (Iwamoto, 2005). A range of perspectives and evaluations stemming from diverse understandings of the Cantonese language and its people have given rise to varied online and real-world practices. After the preceding two chapters have presented an overview of the status of the Cantonese language in Guangdong, as well as the prevailing image of Cantonese people, this chapter shifts its focus to the contents of two Cantonese forums and two Facebook groups after an analysis of videos. Compared with the commercialized talk shows, the posts on these platforms exhibit more personalized, radical, and problem-oriented expressions and opinions. The first two sections explore two Cantonese forums that have been active for nearly 20 years and are based in China, while the subsequent two sections examine two Facebook groups.

Jyut Jyu Baa

Jyut Jyu Baa, as one of the main discussion forums about Cantonese, has attracted over 270,000 followers and generated more than 2,000,000 posts. As a public and free platform to discuss and learn Cantonese, its members are mainly Cantonese supporters.

Figure 4.1: The homepage of Jyut Jyu Baa

Note. The screenshot is captured from Baidu Tieba. Source: https://reurl.cc/p6GXm8

Figure 4.1 displays its homepage with the number of followers and posts as well as the logo, the traditional and ancient writing of "Jyut Jyu Baa." Since the written language used within the forum is mainly simplified Cantonese, only Cantonese speakers and people who know Cantonese can understand the contents. The Baa head (吧主) who is elected by the users and a team of small forum heads manage the forum together. They have the right to recommend and delete posts.

Even though the online forum is not as popular as Weibo, WeChat, BiliBili, and TikTok in mainland China, Jyut Jyu Baa is still a vibrant community with growing followers and posts. Considering the huge number of posts generated by the forum every day, by choosing the posts with at least 10 replies and excluding the irrelevant posts, there are still 190 posts from April 1 to June 30, 2022. At least two posts with more than 10 replies, on average, are posted every day. Table 4.1 calculates the number of posts in each month.

Table 4.1: The Collected Posts from April-June 2022

Month	April	May	June
Number of posts	48	72	70

According to the contents of the collected posts, 12 categories are categorized with examples in Table 4.2. They are the sharing of Cantonese knowledge, news about Cantonese, personal Cantonese experience, and queries, requests, opinions, comments, advocacy, discussion, debate, entertainment, and statements. It is necessary to explain the definition of each category. The query category is usually with questions. Users from non Guangdong provinces, which are shown with the Internet protocol, address ask questions about certain words or phrases' meaning or pronunciation in Cantonese. It is different from the category of request. The request here means asking for help, not for an instant answer. The opinion is that users express their points of view directly, while the comment is created by certain events or opinions with videos, pictures, or voice messages in the post. Comment focuses on a certain issue, and advocacy expresses an action to change.

In the discussion category, the original post invites the members within the forum to join and talk about a topic, but in the debate, one user lists the opinions they disagree with and then refutes them with evidence or opinion. In the last two categories, entertainment is for Cantonese music or operas sharing without a certain purpose, and statement is from the forum head to announce decisions.

Discussion and debate usually do not lead to any conclusions. Jyut Jyu Baa, in general, is a mild community, even though some opinions from several users with ID names are not accepted by the members. Learning Cantonese is the mainstream in the forum. As Table 4.2 shows, the query category has the most posts, with 107. Typical posts under this category, for example, are asking meaning and pronunciation of Cantonese. Such posts always receive active replies from Cantonese speaking members because they would love to help. During the data collection period, the hot spot of the forum was the status of

Gwong Zau Waa (Guangzhou dialect 廣州話) in the Cantonese language family. The users from Guangxi and Guangdong were fighting for the source of Cantonese and the definition of standard Cantonese. Both argued Cantonese stemmed from their hometowns. The topic was so hot that the forum head released four statements to claim the stance to Gwong Zau Waa and the principle of the forum. Meanwhile, the fights also extended to the Gwong Dung Waa Baa since the two forums have common users, though their purposes and principles are different.

Table 4.2: The Categories of Posts from April to June 2022

No.	Category	Example	Number of post
1	knowledge sharing	"The pronunciation comparison among Cantonese's districts from 1 to 10"	23
2	query	"What are the differences between Guangxi Baak Waa and Cantonese?" "How to speak 'guava' in Cantonese?"	107
3	opinion	"As a Hongkonger living in mainland China, I can make an objective judgment that it is reasonable to put Canton's Cantonese as the main theme in the pub…" "You can argue Cantonese merely has 100 years' history, but I can say you are ignorant."	21
4	request	"Is there someone available to teach me Cantonese?"	13
5	discussion	"The verbs of fisting in Cantonese include 'dub', 'cai'…what else…we can discuss more under the post…"	4
6	debate	"This is the logic of the friend from Jiangmen…one disparity overturns the whole…"	2
7	news sharing	"Zeng Xiaomin advised to build a Cantonese protection center of the Guangdong–Hong Kong–Macau Greater Bay Area…"	3
8	entertainment	"Here are the cartoon songs that we fancied in the past."	7
9	advocacy	"Doing something to protect Cantonese is much more important than fighting here…figuring out a solution to preserve Cantonese for the next generation…"	3
10	personal experience	"I went to Tianhe to serve a customer yesterday…I asked a child why he hated to speak Cantonese…he said, 'someone speaking Cantonese is a theft'…"	1
11	comment	"[We] should speak Mandarin like this." "Cantonese people speak Cantonese forever."	2
12	statement	"I announce to dismiss one team member's position to maintain the forum's order…"	4

In the Jyut Jyu Baa, aside from Gwong Zau Waa, other variants of the Cantonese language in Guangdong and Guangxi are shared or discussed. Therefore, Jyut Jyu Baa, in fact, refers to more Cantonese dialects. Since disagreement always exists, the advocacy to put differences aside and focus on the younger generation's Cantonese got the second most responses among 190 posts.

Besides, there are four subthemes under the title. Figure 4.2 shows 4 subthemes and 8 topics under the recommended collection (吧主推薦). Any valuable posts will be recommended and collected by the forum head. On the topic of protecting the mother tongue, there are four pages of posts. Users shared news, news reviews, and their concerns and solutions for Cantonese.

Figure 4.2: The themes under the discussion forum

看贴	图片	吧主推荐	视频	protecting mother tongue
全部	零舍迳典	学习天地	语音及文字	俗语及语法	各地粤语	文化	保卫粤语	大杂烩

Note. The screenshot is captured from Baidu Tieba. Source: https://reurl.cc/gDdl8X

The earliest post was published in 2005, while the latest post was in 2018. Through sorting out these posts, the changes in residents' attitudes to Cantonese and Cantonese environment in Guangdong were recorded clearly. The attacks from non-Cantonese speakers to Cantonese have appeared since 2005. Two years later, there was an advocacy to unite the Cantonese speakers in Guangdong, Guangxi, and beyond China to protect Cantonese, but some replies argued that the advocacy was overreacted. However, more and more expressions about how to protect Cantonese came out in 2008. The rest of the posts were the ideas of promoting Cantonese via individuals, parents, schools, media, and enterprises. Members of the forum are aware that Cantonese is unlikely to become an official language without political power in mainland China. Thus, individual effort is more controllable compared with schools, media, and enterprises. More than four posts' solutions rely on individual actions, including using written Cantonese with a unified Pinyin system online, speaking Cantonese on as many occasions as possible, and supporting Cantonese speaking business owners.

Gwong Dung Waa Baa

Compared with the Jyut Jyu Baa, the number of followers and the posts of Gwong Dung Waa Baa are much smaller. Also, Gwong Dung Waa Baa's topics seem to be more causal, while Jyut Jyu Baa focuses on the language itself and academic discussion. It is very likely that the two forums have common users; even the Baa heads know each other online, but the styles and tones of the forums are not the same. On certain issues, the two forums may have opposing views and engage in arguments. Gwong Dung Waa Baa, for example, insists on Gwong Zau Waa's standard status in the Cantonese language family with more radical and negative opinions. Figure 4.3 shows the homepage of the Gwong Dung Waa Baa with the number of followers (24,729) and posts (452,112). Its logo is the city flower of Guangzhou, namely, cotton tree.

Figure 4.3: The homepage of the Gwong Dung Waa Baa

Note. The screenshot is captured from Baidu Tieba. Source: https://reurl.cc/K0GDxg

Gwong Dung Waa Baa is not as active as the Jyut Jyu Baa. To find out its features, the book collects the posts from 2019 until May 2022. After excluding the deleted and irreverent posts, Table 4.3 shows the number of each year's posts up to 291. The users within the forum also questioned whether the forum has died due to the lack of new posts despite a slow growth in followers. One of the reasons may be the forum's design and rules. If an ID's ranking is too low, the posted content will be deleted upon submission. Even for older IDs, their posts can be removed if they haven't been active for an extended period. This challenge is compounded by the forum's unclear censorship system, which frequently perplexes users. One user felt annoyed after making several edits to a post yet remained confused about why the forum refused to approve it.

Table 4.3: The Collected Posts from 2019-May 2022

Year	2019	2020	2021	Jan-May 2022
Number of posts	106	95	56	34

Table 4.3 shows 15 categories with examples. Similar to the definitions of categories in the Jyut Jyu Baa, Table 4.4 adds four new categories, namely, wish, promotion, greeting, and others except debate. Wish here means the post content is a wish from the members of the forum. Promotion is when members generate posts to advertise their works or accounts about Cantonese. Greeting is for the new members to introduce themselves in the forum. The last category, "others," is none of the above groups but quotations and activity in posts.

As Table 4.4 shows, the query category has the most posts, but the proportion in 291 posts is lower. Instead, the total number of categories of opinion, comment, and personal experience reaches almost half. The members of the Gwong Dung Waa Baa have a stronger desire to observe and express themselves.

Table 4.4: The Categories of Posts from 2019 to May 2022

No.	Category	Example	Number of post
1	opinion	"Aside from Siri, Google assistant also supports Cantonese…technology protects language is available." "I believe Cantonese would be valued with the Greater Bay Area's development."	58
2	comment	"Do you feel shamed as a Cantonese host?" "This is northerner's general view to Cantonese"	64
3	discussion	"…please reply to me how you feel if I create a group to share Cantonese learning resources"	8
4	news sharing	"Yulin will stop the last Cantonese TV program"	2
5	knowledge sharing	"The rarely used Cantonese phrases in my memory"	18
6	query	"How to express 'involution' in Cantonese?" "Is there kindergarten teaching in Cantonese now?"	66
7	advocacy	"[I] hope the users here support our local enterprises."	7
8	entertainment	"[I] share the song 'Coi San Dou.'"	31
9	personal experience	"I drove around in Shaoguan these days and found only the elderly spoke Cantonese…" "I knew one guy whose origin is Sichuan, but he identifies himself as Huizhouist because he can speak 8 dialects…praise him for integration…"	17
10	wish	"One of my new year's wishes is to establish a company which maintains the most advanced manufacture in Lingnan."	4
11	promotion	"You are welcome to visit my channel…I am about to make Cantonese movie clips."	5
12	greeting	"A Cantonese checks in."	1
13	request	"Who has the book 'Cantonese made easy' please?"	2
14	statement	"I am warning someone here not to break the rules…you will pay the cost if you make troubles in the pub."	3
15	others	quotation, activity	5

Even though Gwong Dung Waa Baa has not been active in the number of posts in the past three years, its users' consciousness of Cantonese is very strong. First, they are concerned about Cantonese ups and downs with a high warning mind. For example, the phenomenon of the addition of Mandarin terms into the Cantonese lexicon is prevailing in the young generation. In users' opinions, this is annoying as lots of created Mandarin vocabulary does not make sense and is replacing the original expression in Cantonese.

Second, they use "Laau" (撈) to call the northerners (Beifang Ren 北方人) who do not speak Cantonese. This word appeared many times in the forum to describe the non-Cantonese people and things. To avoid the censorship of the forum, some users used the English word "load" instead, but every Cantonese speaker understands the meaning due to the similar pronunciation. Aside from "Laau," other similar terms used to refer to northerners include Lingbei (嶺北)

and Beilao (北佬), which reflect the popular view that any regions outside of Guangdong province, including the Hainan province, are considered the north. That is why those non-Cantonese speaking immigrants in Guangdong, no matter where they come from, are called northerners.

Figure 4.4: The word cloud of posts' titles

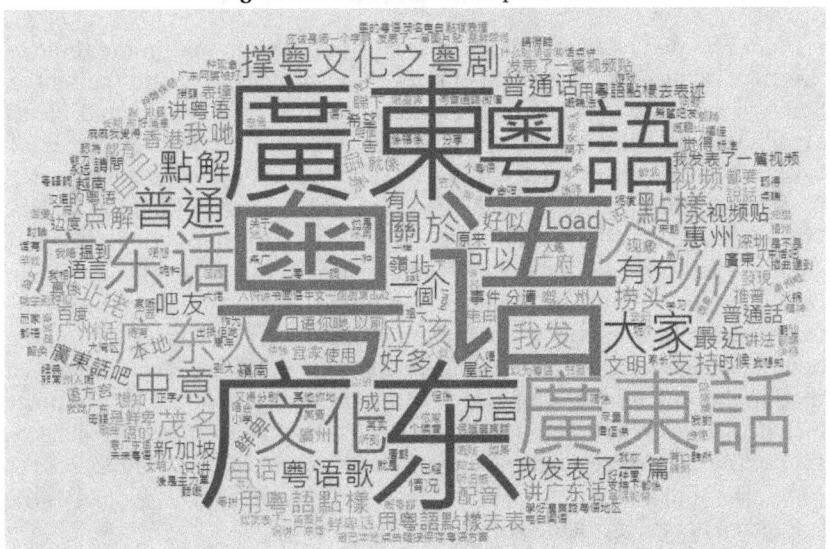

By tallying the word counts in the titles of 291 posts, Figure 4.4 illustrates the frequency of each word. The larger the size, the more frequent the occurrence. It is obvious that Guangdong (廣東) and Cantonese (粵語) occurred the most in posts' titles, but as the book mentioned, "Laau" with "Laau Tau" (撈頭) "Laau Waa" (撈話), "Load" "Lingbei" "Beilao" were used a lot. In recent years, the definition of "Laau" has expanded to include the local second generation who were born and grew up in Guangzhou but do not know how to speak Cantonese. No one within the forum thought the call was inappropriate. In fact, such a call is often viewed as discrimination against non-Cantonese speakers since it has been popular for many years in the Guangdong area. However, considering users' strong localism and the context of the Cantonese crisis, the use of "Laau" here is more about self-protection and setting boundaries between Cantonese and non-Cantonese people than discrimination.

Likewise, there are four subthemes under the forum title. Figure 4.5 shows seven topics under listed in the recommendation collection (吧主推薦). The recommended posts were collected by the forum head, but it seems that they have not been updated in a long time.

Figure 4.5: The themes under the discussion forum

看贴　　图片　　吧主推荐　　视频　　freedom of speech

全部｜公告｜粤语学习｜漫谈粤语｜粤语新闻｜海外粤语｜岭南风光｜百家争鸣

Note. The screenshot is captured from Baidu Tieba. Source: https://reurl.cc/DA0DvR

There was no collection about language protection, but on the topic of "freedom of speech," at least 46 out of 223 posts were related to Cantonese. Some of these posts referred to the rally of 2010. Members' hatred of the Mandarin promotion policy and the ideas to protect Cantonese can be found easily among the posts, such as, "it would be best if Putonghua disappeared from the world…if the northern devils want to exterminate my mother tongue, I will not stand with them in this world…I never view the northern devils as my compatriots," "Mandarin should be withdrawn as the language of education in Guangdong and Cantonese should fully return to school," and "I agree with you that we need to summon overseas Tang people (唐人)[1] to come back to their hometown and start their own business. In this way, we firstly can strengthen the Lingnan people's group and turf the northerners out…" These posts included developing Cantonese literature, issuing laws to protect dialects, supporting Cantonese-speaking business owners, teaching in Cantonese, and so on. The thought of viewing non-Cantonese speakers in Guangdong as the colonizing behavior of a foreign nation appeared in 2009.

In all, despite their different styles, both forums share a similar attitude towards the prospects of Cantonese in Guangdong. These prospects include two main facets. First, when it comes to promoting Cantonese, both forums emphasize the importance of written Cantonese in online communication and literature. As mentioned earlier, Cantonese has its own Pinyin and writing system, but it is not given much value by the government, schools, media, or parents. Using Cantonese is not encouraged in public and formal occasions as it is not considered a standard language. Even at the public events that were organized by local government, TV stations, or schools for the purpose of promoting Cantonese transmission, such as speech competitions or story-telling contests, forum members did not hold high expectations because they believed that the young participants had not formed the habit of using Cantonese and are likely to switch to Mandarin once the event is over.

Similarly, the interviewee Lao Zhenyu responds with the same observation that the efforts like the annual Cantonese-speaking day on July 25 supported

---

[1] Some overseas Cantonese immigrants called themselves Tang people and their hometown as Tang Shan (唐山).

by local middle schools and primary schools are not enough to protect Cantonese, and not all Cantonese-speaking activities such as Cantonese courses, Cantonese story-telling radio shows, Cantonese shows in various forms held or organized by the civil groups in Guangzhou are accepted by the society. For instance, the first Cantonese textbook made by a local primary school was banned as someone from outside of Guangdong reported it to the Ministry of Education for the reason of breaking national unification (Stand News, 2017). In addition, he finds that the influence of mass media is much weaker compared to the situation in 2010. While residents once rallied to protest against Mandarin broadcasting at a local TV station, nowadays, few people care about the number of Cantonese shows or channels on TV.

However, members of the two forums realized the value of a unified written system. They believed that it not only facilitates Cantonese development but also forms a systematic way to learn Cantonese. Hence, in their eyes, Cantonese will not decline if it is being used. Currently, there are mainly six Cantonese romanization systems (Jyutping 粵拼),[2] and the most popular one is from the Linguistic Society of Hong Kong. This means that there is no standardized and widely recognized romanization system in Guangdong. Furthermore, Guangzhou's Cantonese is not completely identical to Hong Kong's Cantonese. When users in both forums type Cantonese, they usually adopt the input methods based on one of the six systems and even explore their own versions of spelling and writing rules with advice and improvement.

Secondly, in contrast to the popular view of a positive and bright imagination regarding the Greater Bay Area project, the collected posts on the project reveal up to 15 posts from the two forums expressing anxieties about Cantonese in the area's development. They fear that Cantonese will be further weakened under the project. The thought was very straightforward; the project, in theory, integrates nine cities of Guangdong and two special administrative regions that share a similar culture and language, but it will attract more and more migrant workers who do not speak Cantonese. Consequently, Mandarin will become the only common language in the area. Furthermore, members realize that they have no right to determine their language and respond with strong critical and doubtful emotions to the policy. Posts like "Do you really believe the saying 'unchanged for 50 years'?" and "The project is useless if the official and teaching language is not Cantonese… don't believe it…" can be seen in their discussions. As a result, they fear that the area will become a bigger Shenzhen that only speaks Mandarin and follows the socialist system with Chinese characteristics.

---

[2] Six systems include the versions from the Linguistic Society of Hong Kong, Guangzhou Dialect, the Education University of Hong Kong, Sidney Lau, Yale romanization, and Hong Kong Government.

Since both forums' members emphasize the role of Cantonese writing, it is meaningful to provide further information on the state of Cantonese writing in Guangzhou. One interviewee, Rao Yuansheng provides insight based on his life experience. His parents are Hakka people, but he was born and grew up in Guangzhou in 1957 and can only speak Gwong Zau Waa (Guangzhou dialect). He is almost one of the earliest Cantonese writers and the main contributor to the well-known short sketch "*Uncle Lok and Haa Zai*" (樂叔和蝦仔).[3] Now, he finds that even the local media from a traditional Cantonese-speaking region can make mistakes in Cantonese writing, not to mention the local TV hosts' children who cannot speak Cantonese. He recalls that the situation began when children's teachers at kindergartens and primary schools could only speak Mandarin. That is why he also runs Cantonese learning projects at a primary school in Guangzhou to improve the situation. As an author who has published books about Cantonese knowledge and diet and made TV shows about Guangdong cultures, he acknowledges that Guangdong did not develop the Cantonese industry well. Although he has written Cantonese since the 1980s, he never learned the Cantonese writing system. Instead, he types Cantonese with handwriting or the input method provided by software on mobile phones. Thus, developing modern Cantonese literature in Guangdong, as the wonderful wish of many members of the Jyut Jyu Baa and the Gwong Dung Waa Baa, and the solution to save Cantonese, is a lengthy and challenging path.

When comparing Hong Kong, a hub where Cantonese is spoken and written, to Guangzhou, it becomes evident that Cantonese has flourished within a free and multicultural environment in Hong Kong. Cantonese characters are prevalent in local newspapers, movie subtitles, instant messaging software, and so on. Moreover, Hong Kong's written Cantonese shows very strong local characteristics by mixing with English and other languages. Thus, it is common that a non-Hong Kong Cantonese speaker may not understand its meaning. Even though Cantonese writing is popular in Hong Kong society, pure Cantonese literature is marginal. But the situation may change with the recently rising localism in Hong Kong. The younger generation in and beyond Hong Kong has launched the first literary magazine of pure Cantonese novels and articles,[4] the first Cantonese writing competition,[5] and campaigns for writing in Cantonese. It remains to be seen what the future holds for the development of Cantonese literature in Hong Kong. Nonetheless, it is doubtless that Hong Kong will get a

---

[3] The introduction of Guangzhou's animation industry can be retrieved at https://culture.china.com/expo/11171063/20190104/34886914_all.html#page_2

[4] The introduction of the magazine can be found at https://resonate.hk/

[5] The writing competition's organizer can be found at https://gongjyuhok.hk/cwdcantoncompo/content

Civil Practices for Cantonese Prospect   59

head start on Guangzhou as well as provide a potential model for the growth of a common language in civil society. After all, Guangzhou's Cantonese also has hybrid characteristics and a writing tradition. If Hong Kong or Guangdong is an independent entity, it is very likely that Cantonese will become a national language with standardized pronunciation and writing rules. Moreover, a proficiency test for non-Cantonese speakers to assess their Cantonese language skills, akin to IELTS, TOEFL, TEL, and JLPT, could be established. In other words, Cantonese is able to become a fully developed language.

Cantonese Revival Zone

The discussion group was founded in 2018 by several individuals of Cantonese origins from Taiwan and Vietnam with the aim of learning and communicating Cantonese among Cantonese and non-Cantonese speakers in the world. The group's name, "The Revival Zone of Canton's Cultures and Languages," also highlights its purpose. Figure 4.6 shows its funny profile photo, the map of Guangdong under the Qing Empire, which bears a resemblance in size and shape to modern-day Guangdong but with different regional divisions. Even though the group has existed for a few years, the number of members is stable at around 900.

Figure 4.6: The profile photo of the Cantonese Revival Zone

Note. The screenshot is captured from its Facebook page. Source: https://www.facebook.com/groups/2234732140147209

As a cultural exchange group, the administrators encourage content about Cantonese culture and music, but they ban all political content to avoid confrontations within the group. To analyze the contents and the characters of the posts within the group, three keywords, Jyut Jyu (粵語), Gwong Dung Waa (廣東話), and Gwong Zau Waa (廣州話)[6], are used to search. There were 155

---

[6] Three key words in the book share the same meaning and are used interchangeably.

related posts from 2018 to May 2022, and the most posts, 78, were generated in 2021.

Table 4.5 lists ten categories: sharing, recommendation, query, request, advocacy, debate, opinion, promotion, creating, and other. In particular, four explicit types of Cantonese knowledge, news, comments, and personal experiences are under the sharing category. It can be seen that sharing is the main content in the group. Cantonese knowledge, including its usage, writing, meaning, and pronunciation, has the most posts, while the original opinions are only five. The knowledge posts or the query posts always receive the most active responses from members. For example, someone asked a question, "Is there a responding translation in Cantonese to the Mandarin 'Ka Bo Zi'?" There were 103 replies under this post.

Table 4.5: Ten Categories of 155 Posts with Examples

No.	Category		Example	Number
1	sharing	Cantonese knowledge	"200 popular Cantonese idioms"	37
		news related to Cantonese	"Cantonese is not only the common language, but also the quintessence of culture in Hong Kong…the Linguistic Society of Hong Kong held a Cantonese reading test on June 15 …"	4
		comments to non-news sources	"It is impressive that the Japanese guy teaches Cantonese."	28
		personal experience	"When I was 10 years old, I made money by providing Cantonese service…"	5
2	recommendation		"You can have a try on the following Mandarin from a Cantonese perspective."	1
3	query		"Is there an easy way to learn Cantonese?"	25
4	request		"Please support my original Cantonese channel."	8
5	advocacy		"Please give a hand to save Sandford's Cantonese class."	5
6	debate		"Peter, don't be silly…these are not Cantonese…you can insist on your opinion…"	2
7	opinion		"Cantonese Americans generally call themselves Tong Jan or Cantonese…Jyut Jyu is called as Tong Waa or Gwong Dung Waa."	5
8	promotion		"You are welcome to register our Cantonese communication activity."	9
9	creating event/poll		"If you meet someone learning Chinese from Virginia, will you correct the state name…please vote…"	2
10	other		quotation or post without expressing anything	24

Since the members focus more on the language and culture, it is not easy to discover their attitudes or stances regarding the status of Cantonese and its relationship with the government. However, their concerns about Cantonese can be seen from the debates on Cantonese writing, the advocacy of online petitions to save Cantonese, and the insistence on using Cantonese, especially for many of them residing in non-Cantonese speaking regions. It can be said that the ban on political topics from the administrators restricts members' further expression and discussion.

Gwong Zau Jan

Compared with the "Cantonese Revival Zone," the Facebook group "Gwong Zau Jan" looks like a different world. It was founded by several Cantonese speakers mainly from the United States and Guangdong, in 2015. One of the administrators, Tony Li, is a Cantonese American who grew up in South America. Tony finds that there are many visible and invisible obstacles to expression in China. Therefore, he runs a discussion group to encourage various opinions and stances, especially political discussions, to gather the people who care about Cantonese. At this point, administrators within the group do not censor members' opinions unless they break the group rules. What's more, the administrators also generate content to have an influence on social media. They manage a non-profit radio channel on YouTube where they organize conversations or interviews on political topics.

Figure 4.7: The profile photo of the Gwong Zau Jan

Note. The screenshot is captured from the Facebook page.
Source: https://www.facebook.com/groups/1501040153535706

Compared with the previously analyzed talk shows in Guangdong, the concern of the discussion group probably is how to make some unconventional and radical opinions, such as Cantonese people's self-governance right and the assumption of building a Cantonese nation, acceptable. As Tony Li said, all opinions, including the extreme ones, are open for review and discussion, even though he does not think that protecting Cantonese is a sensitive issue in

China, as evidenced by the many related articles that are spread on WeChat. The purpose of the group is to provide a free and inclusive platform for anyone who likes Guangdong cultures or has connections with Guangdong to communicate. Even though the name of the group is Gwong Zau Jan (Guangzhou people 廣州人), as Figure 4.7 shows, the shared topics or contents are not limited to Guangzhou. To ensure high-quality discussions and maintain a friendly environment, the group administrators set admission standards by asking questions and limiting the number of members to around 5,000.

Table 4.6: Nine Categories of 228 Posts with Examples

No.	Category		Example	Number
1	sharing	Cantonese knowledge	"If you know the following 200 proverbs, you master Cantonese."	6
		news related to Cantonese	"The Linguistic Society of Hong Kong held a Cantonese reading test on June 15…Dr. Zhan Bohui argued Cantonese is used more than Mandarin and English in Hong Kong…"	11
		comments to non-news sources	"Don't forget the northern Greater China never accepts Cantonese as a part of it…both the national government of ROC and the Communist Party ban Cantonese…"	54
		personal experience	"I always ask my 10-year-old daughter to watch Cantonese children's shows. Meanwhile, my wife and me communicate with her in Cantonese…Everyone is responsible for protecting Cantonese."	51
2	recommendation		"I recommend the restaurant in Gong Yuan Qian, where the store owner speaks Cantonese."	7
3	query		"Where can I find the Cantonese textbooks?"	18
4	request		"Please notify me if you find localized stores in the Guangdong area."	6
5	advocacy		"Speaking Cantonese to be civilized." "We, as the people of Yue country, must continue to pass down Cantonese to the next generation."	8
6	debate		"There is an idiot who did not respect Cantonese…here are his opinions. I disagree…"	8
7	opinion		"I hope that we can still focus on publicizing the Cantonese language and establishing the Cantonese-speaking people overseas so that the world will not confuse the Cantonese-speaking people with the Chinese ethnic group in China."	45
8	promotion		"We need your support for our first WeChat radio station."	5
9	other		quotation or post without expressing anything	9

The group members are mainly from Hong Kong, Guangdong, Vietnam, Malaysia, and Australia. Usually, the members from Hong Kong post and share the most content, while the ones from Guangdong just read or comment. The posted contents are varied, and there are no restrictions in the group. By searching three key words Jyut Jyu (粵語), Gwong Dung Waa (廣東話), and Gwong Zau Waa (廣州話) within the group, there were 228 posts from 2015 to May 2022. The posts' forms were varied on Facebook, with texts or without texts, with links to news, videos, or pictures. Based on the content of these posts, they can be classified into nine categories: sharing, recommendation, query, request, advocacy, debate, opinion, promotion, and other. The biggest number of posts reached 56 in 2016.

In the sharing category, there are four explicit types, as Table 4.6 shows. Members shared Cantonese knowledge, news, comments on certain information with links, pictures, or videos, and personal experiences. The attitudes and emotions toward Cantonese can be acknowledged, especially through personal experiences. In the experiences, members admired and supported the use of Cantonese in formal and informal settings. They appreciated the opportunity to speak with people who can speak fluent and standard Cantonese. Additionally, speaking Cantonese in Cantonese-speaking places is considered normal, whereas not speaking Cantonese in Guangzhou is considered shameful. Therefore, members' preferences and dislikes are clear. They criticized administrators who suppress Cantonese, local parents who abandon Cantonese, and immigrants who refuse to learn Cantonese in Guangdong as foes.

In the opinion category, members tried to propose available solutions to protect and promote Cantonese. For example, the Cantonese people within Guangzhou could take advantage of any chance to speak Cantonese even though they encountered someone who was unable or not willing to speak Cantonese. Meanwhile, social media was a powerful tool to promote Cantonese. Thus, Cantonese speakers within and beyond China could make multiple shows in Cantonese on social media to influence the audience, especially young people, slowly and indirectly.

In addition, the insistence on Cantonese language also contributes to a distinct consciousness. A member of the group argued that since the Cantonese-speaking people have claimed themselves as Tang people (唐人) over the years, there is no concept of overseas Chinese; instead, there are the descendants of the Cantonese and Min people, the descendants of Hong Kong, Macao, and Taiwan, and the descendants of mainlanders. This suggests a division between the Cantonese nation and the Chinese nation.

Furthermore, the bold idea of building a traditional Cantonese country overseas where a development company would collect money and talent from Hong Kong and Guangdong and then purchase land from a foreign government for

Cantonese residents was shared. By charging the management fee from residents, the foreign government/regime would manage the company's security and diplomatic relations. This post provided one possible way to preserve Cantonese and its community and received 64 responses within the group. It was an active and valuable discussion on a political topic among the general public. However, such discussions essentially disappeared after 2016. According to Tony Li's observations, even Hong Kong members reduced their postings after the National Security Law[7] was enacted in 2020.

Taken together, on the one hand, four discussion groups have something in common. Members within each group write or are encouraged to write in Cantonese and acknowledge the decline of Cantonese by expressing anxieties, claiming resolution, and proposing various solutions. They keep a similar attitude and emotion to the culprits who cause Cantonese dying. It is interesting to find that the members of Guangxi and Guangdong fight for the standard Cantonese on the forums, but in Facebook groups, Cantonese speakers unite to target Mandarin and Mandarin speakers, especially on multiple issues by underscoring the shared fate of Guangdong and Hong Kong.

On the other hand, the four groups show different characteristics. The freedom of expression on Facebook is broader. As a discussion platform, "Gwong Zau Jan" provides some bold imagination to a possible Cantonese community while the ideas on the Cantonese forums are confined to the established institution and environment. For example, to develop Cantonese literature, other solutions proposed by forum members seem to reflect the fact that individuals' efforts on Cantonese protection are more reliable than those from the existing government, law, media, and schools in mainland China.

In summary, the role of language in collective identity is more evident in the discussion groups than in the content generation on TV and talk shows. As a Cantonese, speaking and writing Cantonese are the core components. The language here defines a group. Moreover, from their discussions, the distinctions between Cantonese people and people from other parts of China, especially northerners, are recognized and confirmed by members. Harris (1997) defines popular nationalism as a group of people with common cultural attributes who have the authority to manage affairs. Therefore, it may be too early to talk about the formation of a Cantonese nation, but a national consciousness seems to emerge among members.

---

[7] The law is seen as a threat to freedom and the way of life in Hong Kong. Analysis of its impacts can be retrieved at https://www.amnesty.org/en/latest/news/2020/07/hong-kong-national-security-law-10-things-you-need-to-know/.

Besides, several questions left with the members to be further pondered. Since Cantonese is crucial to Cantonese identity, the first question is how to position Cantonese among Chinese languages. If it is viewed as a dialect, as the central government does, it and minority languages will eventually be replaced by Mandarin. Then, the Cantonese identity would not exist. However, if it is viewed as a national language, the measures and efforts taken on it will be different. In other words, the activities of protecting and promoting Cantonese are not necessary to bond with CCP's state nationalism. For example, for the interviewee Lao Zhenyu, the purpose of protecting and promoting Cantonese was to maintain the diverse Chinese cultures, which is a common view in mainland China, but for the interviewee Tony Li, the term "Chinese" (Zhong Hua 中華) refers to the ruling class in history. As Cantonese is considered a dialect in the modern era, protecting or inheriting Chinese cultures actually means promoting Mandarin. Therefore, Tony disagrees that Cantonese is a part of Chinese cultures.

The first question thus leads to the second question of how to handle the relationship between Cantonese identity and Chinese identity. As pointed out by Ray (1998), the development of national languages is related to the emergence of a sense of nationhood. However, sharing a common language cannot guarantee a shared sense of nationhood. It is only when language becomes politicized that the struggle for national identity begins (Ray, 1998). China's history has proved that the regime rejects tolerating separation and secession, while Hong Kong's case shows that holding dual identities is unsustainable. The conflicts of two identities also bring up the third question: how to solve the tensions between Cantonese speakers and Mandarin speakers in cultures, values, and lifestyles. Guangdong's policy and economy have been attracting migrant workers from other parts of China since the 1980s. Obviously, migrants have their own languages and life habits. With the aging population, economic slowdown, and negative impact of the pandemic, problems and crises such as unemployment or inflation would surface. Once the conflicts between Cantonese and non-Cantonese for resources and interests break out, the damage to society is huge.

Going back to the language, Cantonese has its merits and limitations. First, it has a vast overseas network around the globe. As Chatterjee (1993) notes, the spiritual domain of a nation, such as language and religion, cannot be changed as easily as the material domain. The inhabitants of Guangdong and immigrants overseas still preserve many original habits, rituals, and principles. Cantonese, as the most common tie, links Cantonese speakers and migrants of Guangdong origin in the world. Creators' visual and audio generation appeal to readers' or viewers' memories and experiences related to Cantonese, and vice versa. Therefore, a pan-Cantonese imagination toward each other is being built up. Also, when the internet becomes a competing sphere of multiple narratives, the diaspora's discourses not only influence but also bypass official censorship. For those diaspora Cantonese, it is meaningless to insist on the pure Cantonese accent and usage. Considering the restrictions and suppression of Cantonese development in China, Cantonese will be preserved and spread overseas in a free and borderless manner. Hence, a narrow nationalism only harms Cantonese development. From the perspective of a loose definition, anyone who can speak Cantonese, regardless of their accents, and share some common attributes can hold a Gwong Dung Jan (people of Guangdong 廣東人) identity.

Second, the limitation: most influential Cantonese vocabularies are limited to life and economy, with many words from Hong Kong. That is to say, the original Cantonese vocabulary in other fields, particularly in politics, is either absent or ignored. Since the nineteenth century, English-language academic works have been translated into Chinese and Japanese. Chinese intellectuals tried to introduce and create new vocabularies which do not exist in ancient Chinese. However, the most commonly used Chinese vocabulary in political systems and governance comes from Japanese,[8] such as politics (政治), revolution (革命), government (政府), party (黨), democracy (民主) and policy (政策). Additionally, Japanese continues to have a significant influence on popular culture today. Thus, in terms of the impact on the creation and translation of modern words, Cantonese has limited power when compared to English and Japanese.

---

[8] The general introduction of Japanese impact on Chinese vocabulary can be found at http://www.cctss.org/article/headlines/4006 and http://www.personpsy.org/Info/Details/2289

Limitation and Conclusion

By reviewing the formation and development of Chinese nationalism, it can be seen that Chinese intellectuals and governors have emphasized and reinforced the role of a unified language. The development of Mandarin has a close relationship with Chinese nation-building, while dialects seem more like obstacles to a stable multinational regime and are at risk of dying out. Although Anderson (2006, p. 135) argues that a nation can still be imagined without linguistic communality, the case of China reflects the crucial role of language in its nation-building. Based on this premise, the internet and other communication technologies are beneficial in deferring the demise of dialects and bringing about new changes, which inspires dialect protectors to develop their mother tongues with new ideas and tools. Therefore, eight cases of the book present Cantonese speakers' efforts and imagination.

The book explores the potential of a virtual Cantonese community by examining the content generation about Cantonese and Cantonese people on TV and digital media. It argues that the awareness of protecting the mother tongue and the doubt toward national policies have been raised among the residents in Guangdong. Through daily practices of Cantonese knowledge, history, common memories, and experiences, Cantonese is preserved, spread, and even evolves with new features on the internet. Even though censorship and self-censorship exist online, dialects receive more space than Mandarin due to language barriers. Moreover, the Cantonese overseas network helps to bypass censorship and expand Cantonese development. That is to say, the particular solidarities of the Cantonese language can connect various Cantonese-speaking groups and regions and imagine each other. Cantonese spoken in Guangzhou, Hong Kong, Macau, Kuala Lumpur, San Francisco, Melbourne, Vancouver, and Sao Paulo can be mutually understood despite variations in features. This linguistic connection fosters a higher level of common memory, culture, and belonging among the Cantonese-speaking communities. More importantly, the findings of eight cases demonstrate the critical role of language in a group that Cantonese people should know how to speak and write Cantonese. From Cantonese users' creation and discussions, the distinctions between Cantonese people and northerners are recognizable, but further questions such as double identities and intergroup tension remain hidden risks. In addition, it should be noted that the impacts of the internet on Cantonese speakers are still difficult to quantify, and predicting the future actions of Cantonese users in Guangdong remains challenging.

The book primarily focuses on the Cantonese group within Guangdong, so one limitation is choosing eight visual-based and textual-based cases of recent years to observe and analyze while there are numerous Cantonese creations and discourses on diverse platforms in the Chinese and English internet. Hence, the landscape of Cantonese online may not be fully represented. Additionally, Cantonese, in fact, is being used in Hong Kong and overseas. Particularly, Hong Kong Cantonese and Guangzhou Cantonese have been evolving in different directions since 1949. The advocacy of using the name "Hong Kong Waa" (香港話) to replace Cantonese as Hongkongers' mother tongue has appeared (Lian, 2023). As a result, other digital practices with local characteristics and history may be different from the cases of the book but contribute to the diversification of Cantonese development. If people acknowledge Cantonese's historical golden ages, such as its role as the primary communication language between Guangzhou residents and foreign businessmen from 1759 to 1842 and its domination in Cantopop cultures during the 1980s to 1990s, the creations and digital practices showcased in the book can be seen as an act of remaking Cantonese and reshaping the image of Cantonese people globally through the power of internet communication technologies.

Cantonese people have successfully spread their culture around the world, with Cantonese cuisine being one of the most popular examples. Initially operated by working-class migrants, Cantonese restaurants and food courts can now be found worldwide. However, unlike the relatively stable cuisine, cultural products, for example, language shows, require more creativity, imagination, various forms, high-level packaging, and widespread visibility. In the era of cultural globalization, Cantonese, as a product of cultural hybridization, is receptive to internationalization and has experience in managing multiple cultures in history. Therefore, new forms and new developments of Cantonese creation with technologies within and beyond Guangdong are likely to be expected, although the challenge is tough, and the responsibility is heavy for the educated and action-oriented generation.

Guangdong is often considered a special place in China. Since the late Qing dynasty, it has been the site of many groundbreaking explorations in education, culture, economic models, and political systems that are well-known, as well as the practices of localists such as the intellectual Ou Jujia, the warlords Chen Jiongming and Chen Jitang, which are less known. Ultimately, this book does not predict the future of the Cantonese language and the identity of Cantonese people but rather aims to be early research on Cantonese from a non-linguistic perspective. It hopes that in the future, in addition to language, there will be more studies of grassroots practices in Guangdong.

References

Anderson, B. (1991, 2006). *Imagined communities: reflections on the origins and spread of nationalism*. London: Verso.

Bainbridge, J. (2011). Textual Analysis and Media Research. In J. Bainbridge, N. Goc, and Tynan (Eds.), *Media and Journalism: New approaches to theory and practice* (pp. 229-242). Australia: Oxford University Press.

Bauer, R. (2018). Cantonese as written language in Hong Kong. *Global Chinese*, 4(1), 103-142. https://doi.org/10.1515/glochi-2018-0006

BBC. (2011, December 18). 廣東頒佈規定限制使用方言 [Guangdong issued regulation to restrict the use of dialect]. *BBC News*. https://www.bbc.com/zhongwen/simp/chinese_news/2011/12/111218_guangdong_dialect_putonghua

Bloomfield, L. (1935). *Language*. New York: HarperCollins.

Bowen, G. A. (2009). Document Analysis as a Qualitative Research Method. *Research Journal*, Vol. 9 No. 2, pp. 27-40. https://doi.org/10.3316/QRJ0902027

Branigan, T. (2010, July 25). Protesters gather in Guangzhou to protect Cantonese language. *The Guardian*. https://www.theguardian.com/world/2010/jul/25/protesters-guangzhou-protect-cantonese

Cabestan, J. P. (2005). The Many Facets of Chinese Nationalism. *China Perspectives*, 59. http://journals.openedition.org/chinaperspectives/2793

Calhoun, C. (2007). *Nations Matter: Culture, History, and the Cosmopolitan Dream*. Routledge: London and New York.

Carrico, K. (2012). Recentering China: The Cantonese in the beyond the Han. In T. S. Mullaney, J. Leibold, S. Gros, and E. Vanden Bussche (Eds.), *Critical Han Studies: The History, Representation, and Identity of China's Majority* (pp. 23-44). University of California Press.

Castells, M. (2004). *The Power of Identity: The Information Age Economy, Society and Culture*. Volume II. Blackwell Oxford.

Census and Statistics Department. (2022, February). Population census: summary results. https://www.censtatd.gov.hk/en/data/stat_report/product/B1120106/att/B11201062021XXXXB01.pdf

Chang, M. H. (2001). *Return Of the Dragon: China's Wounded Nationalism* (1st ed.). Routledge. https://doi.org/10.4324/9780429497636

Chang, S., & Zhuang, C. S. (2008). Geographical distribution of Guangdong dialects: their linkage with natural and historical geography. *Journal of Chinese Studies*, 48, 407-422.

Chatterjee, P. (1993). *Whose Imagined Community? In the Nation and Its Fragments: Colonial and Postcolonial Histories* (1st ed.), 3–13. New Jersey: Princeton University Press

Che, C., & Chien, C. A. (2022, November 29). Memes, puns and blank sheets of paper: China's creative acts of protest. *The New York Times*. https://cn.nytimes.com/china/20221129/china-protests-blank-sheets/zh-hant/dual/

Chen, H. (2020, August 31). The only Mongolian-language social media site was shut down in China. *Vice.* https://www.vice.com/en/article/xg8p7n/the-only-mongolian-language-social-media-site-was-shut-down-in-china

Chen, L. (2023, January 16). The prequel and progression of White Paper Movement: Chinese dissidents identify each other in solitude. *Freedom Asia Radio.* https://www.rfa.org/mandarin/zhuanlan/baodaozheshijian/mrpt-01132023123136.html

Chen, P. (1999). *Modern Chinese: History and Sociolinguistics.* Cambridge: Cambridge University Press.

Chen, X., Xie, J., Wang, Z., Shen, B., & Zhou, Z. (2023). How we express ourselves freely: censorship, self-censorship, and anti-censorship on a Chinese social media. In I. Sserwanga, et al. *Information for a Better World: Normality, Virtuality, Physicality, Inclusivity.* iConference 2023. Lecture Notes in Computer Science, Vol. 13972. Springer, Cham. https://doi.org/10.1007/978-3-031-28032-0_8

Ching, M. B. (2006). 地域文化與國家認同：晚清以來廣東文化觀的形成 [*Regional Culture and National Identity: The Formation of the notion of "Guangdong Culture" since the late Qing*]. Beijing: Joint Publishing

Chiu, C. K. (2020, September 29). 粵讀古詩文 [Cantonese reading of ancient poetry]. *Ta Kung Pao.* https://www.tkww.hk/epaper/view/newsDetail/1310663635835686912.html

Ci, W. (2015, May). 粵語的政治 [The Politics of Cantonese]. *Cultural Studies.* https://www.ln.edu.hk/mcsln/archive/46th_issue/key_concept_01.shtml

Culpepper, R. (2012). Nationalist competition on the internet: Uyghur diaspora versus the Chinese state media. *Asian Ethnicity*, 13(2), pp. 187-203. DOI:10.1080/14631369.2012.625711

De Francis, J. (1950). *Nationalism and Language Reform in China.* Princeton, NJ: Princeton University Press.

deLisle, J., Goldstein, A., & Yang, G. (2016). Introduction. In J. deLisle, A. Goldstein, and G. Yang (Eds.), *The internet, social media, and a changing China.* University of Pennsylvania Press. http://www.jstor.org/stable/j.ctt1b3t8nr

Doyle, A. (2022, May 28). What is a semi-structured interview? *The Balance.* https://www.thebalancecareers.com/what-is-a-semi-structured-interview-2061632

Elo, S., & Kyngas, H. (2008). The qualitative content analysis process. *Journal of advanced nursing*, 62, 107-115. http://dx.doi.org/10.1111/j.1365-2648.2007.04569.x

Fang, K., & Repnikova, M. (2018). Demystifying "Little Pink": The creation and evolution of a gendered label for nationalistic activists in China. *New Media & Society*, 20(6), 2162–2185. https://doi.org/10.1177/1461444817731923

Feng, A., & Adamson, B. (2019). Language policies in education in the People's Republic of China. In A. Kirkpatrick, and A. J. Liddicoat (Eds.), *The Routledge International Handbook of Language Education Policy in Asia.* p. 45-59. Routledge. https://doi.org/10.4324/9781315666235

Fico, F, G., Lacy, S., & Riffe, D. (2008). A content analysis guide for media economics scholars. *Journal of Media Economics*, 21(2), 114-130, Doi: 10.1080/08997760802069994

References

Fok, L. K., & Ma, L. H. (2018, January 16). Falling numbers of Cantonese speakers in Hong Kong spark fears for the future. *Radio Free Asia*. https://www.rfa.org/english/news/china/hongkong-cantonese-01162018062603.html/

Fong, V. (2004). Filial nationalism among Chinese teenagers with global identities. *American Ethnologist*, 31(4), 631–648. http://www.jstor.org/stable/4098872

Friedman, E. (1994). Reconstructing China's national identity: a Southern alternative to Mao- era anti-imperialist nationalism. *The Journal of Asian Studies*, 53(1), 67–91. https://doi.org/10.2307/2059527

Fu, K., Chan, H., & Chau, M. (2013). Assessing censorship on microblogs in China: discriminatory keyword analysis and the real-name registration policy. *IEEE Internet Computing*, 17(3), 42-50, Doi: 10.1109/MIC.2013.28.

Gan, N. (2020, September 5). How China's new language policy sparked rare backlash in Inner Mongolia. CNN. https://www.cnn.com/2020/09/05/asia/china-inner-mongolia-intl-hnk-dst/index.html

Gao, X. (2012). "Cantonese is not a dialect": Chinese netizens' defense of Cantonese as a regional lingua franca. *Journal of Multilingual and Multicultural Development*, 33:5, 449-464, DOI: 10.1080/01434632.2012.680461

Gao, X. (2015). The ideological framing of 'dialect': an analysis of mainland China's state media coverage of 'dialect crisis' (2002–2012). *Journal of Multilingual and Multicultural Development*, 36:5, 468-482, DOI: 10.1080/01434632.2014.943234

Gao, Z. (2012). Chinese grassroots nationalism and its impact on foreign brands. *Journal of Macromarketing*, 32(2), 181–192. https://doi.org/10.1177/0276146711428808

Gellner, E. (1983). *Nations and nationalism*. London: Basil Blackwell.

George, T. (2022, January 27). Semi-structured interview: definition, guide & examples. *Scribbr*. https://www.scribbr.com/methodology/semi-structured-interview/

Gerring, J. (2006). *Case study research: principles and practices*. Cambridge University Press. https://doi.org/10.1017/CBO9780511803123

Gerring, J. (2011). The case study: what it is and what it does. In C. Boix, and S. C. Stokes (Eds.), *The Oxford Handbook of Comparative Politics*. https://doi.org/10.1093/oxfordhb/9780199566020.003.0004

Goldman, M., Link, P., & Wei, S. (1993). China's intellectuals in the Deng era: loss of identity with the state. In L. Dittmer and S. S. Kim (Eds.), *China's Quest for National Identity* (pp. 125–153). Cornell University Press.

Goodman, D. S. G. (1994). The politics of regionalism: economic development, conflict and negotiation. In D. S. G. Goodman, and G. Segal (Eds.), *China Deconstructs: Politics, Trade and Regionalism*. Routledge. https://doi.org/10.4324/9780203038819

Goodman, D. S. G., & Feng, C. (1994). Guangdong: Greater Hong Kong and the new regionalist future. In D. S. G. Goodman, and G. Segal (Eds.), *China Deconstructs: Politics, Trade and Regionalism*. Routledge. https://doi.org/10.4324/9780203038819

Graham, E. J. (2002). 50 years on, 20 years on: revolution and reform in Guangdong. *Asian Geographer*, 21(1-2), 125-144, DOI:10.1080/10225706.2002.9684089

Greenfeld, L., and J. Eastwood. (2009). National Identity. In C. Boix, and S. C. Stokes (Eds.), *The Oxford Handbook of Comparative Politics*. https://doi.org/10.1093/oxfordhb/9780199566020.003.0011

Grzywacz, A. (2012). The role of language in nation-building process. *Jurnal Linguistik Terapan*, 2(2). https://jurnal.polinema.ac.id/index.php/jlt/article/view/247/137

Guo, L. (2004). The relationship between Putonghua and Chinese dialects. In: Zhou, M., Sun, H. (eds) Language Policy in the People's Republic of China. Language Policy, vol 4. Springer, Dordrecht. https://doi.org/10.1007/1-4020-8039-5_3

Guo, L. (2022, August 22). Japanese restaurant Sushiro bans staff from speaking Cantonese. *That's*. https://www.thatsmags.com/guangzhou/post/34930/japanese-restaurant-sushiro-bans-staff-from-speaking-cantonese

Guo, S. H. (2020). *The evolution of the Chinese internet: creative visibility in the digital public*. Stanford University Press. https://doi.org/10.1515/9781503614444

Guo, X., & Yang, S. (2019). Memetic communication and consensus mobilization in the cyber nationalist movement. In L. Hailong (Ed.), *From Cyber-Nationalism to Fandom Nationalism: The Case of Diba Expedition In China* (1st ed.). Routledge. https://doi.org/10.4324/9780429447754

Guo, Y. (2003). *Cultural Nationalism in Contemporary China* (1st ed.). Routledge. https://doi.org/10.4324/9780203300480

Harris, P. (1997). Chinese Nationalism: The State of the Nation. *The China Journal*, 38, 121–37. https://doi.org/10.2307/2950337.

Harrison, J. (1969). *Modern Chinese nationalism*. Hunter College of the City of New York, Research Institute of Modern Asia, New York.

Hastings, A. (1997). *The construction of nationhood: ethnicity, religion and nationalism (The Wiles Lectures)*. Cambridge: Cambridge University Press. Doi:10.1017/CBO9780511612107

He, H. F. (2018, March 12). Why has Cantonese fallen out of favour with Guangzhou youngsters? *South China Morning Post*. https://www.scmp.com/news/china/society/article/2136237/why-has-cantonese-fallen-out-favour-guangzhou-youngsters

He, H. F. (2018, October 21). Meet the Cantonese activist fighting to keep the language alive in its southern Chinese heartland. *South China Morning Post*. https://www.scmp.com/news/china/society/article/2169520/meet-cantonese-activist-fighting-keep-language-alive-its-southern

Ho, W. C., & Lu, J. (2019). Culture versus the state? The "Defend-My-Mother-Tongue" protests in Guangzhou. *China Journal*, 81(1), 81-102. https://doi.org/10.1086/699253

Horsley, J. P. (2022, August 8). Behind the facade of China's cyber super-regulator. *DigiChina*. https://digichina.stanford.edu/work/behind-the-facade-of-chinas-cyber-super-regulator/

Hoshur, S. (2021, January 29). Uyghur language instruction absent from schools in Xinjiang's Kelpin County. *Radio Free Asia*. https://www.rfa.org/english/news/uyghur/language-01292021173514.html

Hu, G. (2018, October 29). Light music team pioneers the trend and music cafe breeds pop new sound. *Jiemian*. https://www.jiemian.com/article/2575221.html

References

Huang, Y. (2021). Canton's unease: as Mandarin spreads, locals face identity crisis. *Sixth Tone*. https://www.sixthtone.com/news/1008922/cantons-unease-as-mandarin-spreads%2C-locals-face-identity-crisis

Initium Media. (2021, August 5). 以「網絡安全」為名：中國網信辦是如何變成一頭巨獸的？[In the name of cyber security: how the cyberspace administration of China becomes a great beast?] https://theinitium.com/article/20210805-mainland-china-cyberspace-administration-rises/

Ip, I. (2010, August 8). 「撐粵語」運動背後的「推普」政治 [The Mandarin promotion politics behind the "shore up Cantonese" movement]. Inmediahk. https://www.inmediahk.net/node/1007938

Iwamoto, N. (2005). The role of language in advancing nationalism. *Research Institute for Humanities Bulletin*, 38, 91-113.

Ji, F. (2018). Language planning and policy in China: unity, diversity and social control. In E. Andrews (Eds.), *Language Planning in the Post-Communist Era*. Palgrave Macmillan, Cham. https://doi.org/10.1007/978-3-319-70926-0_3

Jian, L. (2016, July 21). 陳星：從《城事特搜》到《誰語爭鋒》的綻放 [The interview with Chenxing]. *Gznf*. https://www.gznf.net/event/13137.html

Kuang, W. (2018). *Social media in China*. Singapore: Palgrave Macmillan.

Lacy, S., Watson, B. R., Riffe, D., & Lovejoy, J. (2015). Issues and best practices in content analysis. *Journalism & Mass Communication Quarterly*, 92(4), 791-811. doi:10.1177/1077699015607338

Lai, C. (2021, January 29). Is Cantonese losing its mainstream status in Macao? *The Macao News*. https://macaonews.org/deepdives/is-cantonese-losing-its-mainstream-status-in-macao/

Lam, A. S. L. (2005). *Language Education in China. Policy and Experience from 1949*. Hong Kong University Press, Hong Kong.

Lam, A. S. L. (2008). Language Education Policy in Greater China. In N. H. Hornberger (Eds.), *Encyclopedia of Language and Education*. Springer, Boston, MA. https://doi-org.ezproxy.library.uvic.ca/10.1007/978-0-387-30424-3_30

Lau, M. (2014, July 25). Guangzhou locals seek 'Cantonese Day' to help preserve mother tongue. *South China Morning Post*. https://www.scmp.com/news/china/article/1558497/guangzhou-locals-seek-cantonese-day-help-preserve-mother-tongue

Lee, S. (2016). Surviving online censorship in China: three satirical tactics and their impact. *The China Quarterly*, 228, 1061–1080. http://www.jstor.org/stable/26291589

Li, H. (2017, January 31). 廣東人的由來和組成 [The source and components of Guangdong People]. *Yangcheng Gonglue*. https://m.sohu.com/n/479736857/

Li, H. (2018). Understanding Chinese nationalism: A historical perspective. In L. Hailong (Ed.), *From Cyber-Nationalism to Fandom Nationalism: The Case of Diba Expedition in China* (pp. 125-147). Routledge.

Li, H., & Yuan, Y. (2013). Comparison and contrast of English language planning and policy for senior secondary education between Mainland China and Hong Kong. *Asia-Pacific Edu Res*, 22(4), 439–447. DOI 10.1007/s40299-012-0043-z

Li, X. (1994). 廣東的方言 [Guangdong's Dialects]. Guangdong People Publishing: Guangzhou.

Li, Y. M. (2011). 清末民初的粵語書寫 [*The Cantonese writing between the period of late Qing and the Republic of China*]. Joint Publishing.

Lian, J. (2023, June 2). 香港人的母語老早就不再是廣東話 [Hongkonger's mother tongue has not been Cantonese anymore]. *Freedom Asia Radio*. https://www.rfa.org/cantonese/commentaries/jl/com-06022023082945.html

Liu, H. (2018). Love your nation the way you love an idol: new media and the emergence of fandom nationalism. In L. Hailong (Ed.), *From Cyber-Nationalism to Fandom Nationalism: The Case of Diba Expedition In China* (pp. 125-147). Routledge.

Liu, J. (2019). From mobilization to legitimation: digital media and the evolving repertoire of contention in contemporary China. In *Handbook of Protest and Resistance in China*. Cheltenham, UK: Edward Elgar Publishing.

Liu, Z. (1993). 論普通話的確立和推廣 [The discussion of Putonghua's confirmation and promotion]. *Shanghai Open University*. https://yuyan.shou.org.cn/2018/0515/c7542a59930/page.htm

Lorentzen, P. (2014). China's strategic censorship. *American Journal of Political Science*, 58(2), 402–414. http://www.jstor.org/stable/24363493

Luqiu, R. L. (2018) Counter-hegemony: grassroots use of the Internet to save dialects in China. *Journal of Multilingual and Multicultural Development*, 39(8), 663-674, DOI: 10.1080/01434632.2017.1422738

Miao, W., & Lei, W. (2016). Policy review: the cyberspace administration of China. *Global Media and Communication*, 12(3), 337–340. https://doi.org/10.1177/1742766516680879

Miao, W., Jiang, M., & Pang, Y. (2021). Historicizing Internet Regulation in China: A Meta-Analysis of Chinese Internet Policies (1994-2017). *International journal of communication* [Online], 2003. Gale Literature Resource Center.

Ministry of Education. (1992, September 2). 中國漢語水平考試辦法 [The Solution of Hanyu Shuiping Kaoshi]. http://www.moe.gov.cn/jyb_xxgk/xxgk/zhengce/guizhang/202112/t20211206_585031.html

Ministry of education. (2021, June 2). 粵港澳大灣區語言生活狀況報告 [The report of the language usage in life of the greater bay area]. http://www.moe.gov.cn/fbh/live/2021/53486/sfcl/202106/t20210602_534892.html

Modongal, S. (2016). Development of nationalism in China. *Cogent Social Sciences*, 2(1), DOI: 10.1080/23311886.2016.1235749

Morgan, H. (2022). Conducting a qualitative document analysis. *The Qualitative Report*, 27(1), 64-77. https://doi.org/10.46743/2160-3715/2022.5044

Ng, D, F., & Zhao, J. (2015). Investigating Cantonese speakers' language attitudes in Mainland China. *Journal of Multilingual and Multicultural Development*, 36:4, 357-371, DOI: 10.1080/01434632.2014.925906

Nyíri, P., Zhang, J., & Varrall, M. (2010). China's cosmopolitan nationalists: "heroes" and "traitors" of the 2008 Olympics. *China Journal*, (63), 25-55.

Ozkirimli, U. (2010). *Theories of nationalism: a critical introduction*. Palgrave Macmillan.

References

Ray, T. (1998) Nations and language-building: old theories, contemporary cases. *Nationalism and Ethnic Politics*, 4(3), 79-101. DOI: 10.1080/13537119808428539

Rejai, M., and C. Enloe. (1969). Nation-States and State-Nations. *International Studies Quarterly*, 13(2), 140-158. https://doi.org/10.2307/3013942

Roberts, M. (2018). *Censored: Distraction and Diversion Inside China's Great Firewall*. Princeton: Princeton University Press.

Rohsenow, J. S. (2004). Fifty Years of Script and Written Language Reform in the P.R.C. In M. Zhou, H. Sun (Eds.), *Language Policy in the People's Republic of China. Language Policy*, Vol. 4. Springer, Dordrecht. https://doi.org/10.1007/1-4020-8039-5_2

Rosen, J. (2022, December 23). How do you protest in the face of censorship? An empty sign. *The New York Times*. https://cn.nytimes.com/china/20221223/white-paper-protests-censorship/zh-hant/dual/

Saillard, C. (2004). On the promotion of Putonghua in China: how a standard language becomes a vernacular. In M. Zhou, and H. Sun (Eds.), *Language Policy in the People's Republic of China. Language Policy*, Vol. 4. Springer, Dordrecht. https://doi.org/10.1007/1-4020-8039-5_9

Shen, S. (2007). *Redefining Nationalism in Modern China: Sino–American Relations and the Emergence of Chinese Public Opinion in the 21st Century*. New York: Palgrave Macmillan.

Shu, C. (2017, August 27). China doubles down on real-name registration laws, forbidding anonymous online posts. *TechCrunch*. https://techcrunch.com/2017/08/27/china-doubles-down-on-real-name-registration-laws-forbidding-anonymous-online-posts/

Skarbek, D. (2020). Qualitative research methods for institutional analysis. *Journal of Institutional Economics*, 16(4), 409-422. doi:10.1017/S174413741900078X

Snow, D. (2013) Towards a theory of vernacularisation: insights from written Chinese vernaculars. *Journal of Multilingual and Multicultural Development*, 34(6), 597-610. DOI: 10.1080/01434632.2013.786082

Sonmez, F. (2014, August 25). China is forcing its biggest Cantonese-speaking region to speak Mandarin. *Agence France Presse*. https://www.businessinsider.com/china-is-forcing-its-biggest-cantonese-speaking-region-to-speak-mandarin-2014-8

Stand News. (2017, January 17). 廣州小學編廣東話教材，網民斥「不利國家統一」向教育部舉報 [Guangzhou elementary school's Cantonese textbook was denounced by netizens as "detrimental to national unity" and reported to the Ministry of Education]. https://collection.news/thestandnews/articles/48929

Statistics and Census Service. (2017). Detailed results of 2016 population by-census. https://www.dsec.gov.mo/Intercensos2016/home.aspx?lang=zh-MO

Study Times. (2021, June 14). 中國共產黨與中華民族偉大復興 [The Chinese Communist Party and the revival of Chinese nation]. https://www.cas.cn/zt/sszt/ds/mt/202106/t20210615_4793228.shtml

Sullivan, J., & Wang, W. (2022). China's 'Wolf Warrior Diplomacy': the interaction of formal diplomacy and cyber-nationalism. *Journal of Current Chinese Affairs*, 52(1). https://doi.org/10.1177/18681026221079841

Sun, Z. (2022). Let Dr Ai's story flee: a minor practice against China's internet censorship during the COVID-19 pandemic. *Visual Studies*. DOI:10.1080/1472586X.2022.2070535

Tabouret-Keller, A. (1998). Language and Identity. In F. Coulmas (Ed.), *The Handbook of Sociolinguistics*. Blackwell.

Tai, Q. (2014). China's media censorship: a dynamic and diversified regime. *Journal of East Asian Studies*, 14(2), 185-210. doi:10.1017/S1598240800008900

Tang, Z. (2005, November 16). 論二十世紀末粵語對漢語和漢文化的影響 [A discussion of Cantonese influence on Chinese language and Chinese culture at the end of twentieth century]. http://www.huayuqiao.org/articles/tangzhixiang/tang03.htm

The Paper. (2019, November 15). 廣東三大方言是如何形成的? [How to form three major dialects of Guangdong?] https://www.thepaper.cn/newsDetail_forward_4911028

The People's Daily. (1955). 爲促進漢字改革、推廣普通話、實現漢語規範化而努力 [Striving to reform Chinese characters, promote Mandarin, and standardize the Chinese language]. https://cn.govopendata.com/renminribao/1955/10/26/1/#131639

Tomlinson, J. (2007). Globalization and cultural analysis. In A. Mcgrew, and D. Held (Eds.), *Globalization Theory: Approaches and Controversies* (p. 148–165). Polity.

Townsend, J. (1992). Chinese Culturalism. *The Australian Journal of Chinese Affairs*, 27, 97-130.

Vergani, M., & Zuev, D. (2011). Analysis of YouTube videos used by activists in the Uyghur Nationalist Movement: combining quantitative and qualitative methods. *Journal of Contemporary China*, 20(69), 205-229. DOI: 10.1080/10670564.2011.541628

Wan, D. (2014). The history of language planning and reform in China: a critical perspective. *Working Papers in Educational Linguistics (WPEL)*, 29 (2). https://repository.upenn.edu/wpel/vol29/iss2/5

Wang, J. (2006). The politics of goods: a case study of consumer nationalism and media discourse in Contemporary China. *Asian Journal of Communication*, 16(2), 187-206. DOI: 10.1080/01292980600638710

Wang, R. (2015). Engaging Government for Environmental Collective Action: Political Implications of ICTs in Rural China. In W. Chen, and S. D. Reese (Eds.), *Networked China: Global Dynamics of Digital Media and Civic Engagement: New Agendas in Communication* (1st ed.). Routledge. https://doi.org/10.4324/9781315733074

Wang, Z. (2014). The Chinese dream: concept and context. *Journal of Chinese Political Science*, 19, 1–13. https://doi.org/10.1007/s11366-013-9272-0

Wang, Z. (2018). "We are all Diba members tonight": cyber-nationalism as emotional and playful actions online. In L. Hailong (Ed.), *From Cyber-Nationalism to Fandom Nationalism: The Case of Diba Expedition in China* (pp. 53-71). Routledge.

Weatherley, R., & Zhang, Q. (2017). *History and nationalist legitimacy in contemporary China: a double-edged sword*. Palgrave Macmillan: London.

References

Wu, D. (2022, November 24). A trial of Mandarin test for primary and middle school students starting from December 15. *Xinhua*. http://www.news.cn/politics/202211/24/c_1129154669.htm

Wu, H. (2020, March 5). Tibetan language learning eroded under China's "bilingual education": rights group. *Reuters*. https://www.reuters.com/article/us-china-education-tibet-idUSKBN20S13W

Wu, X., & Fitzgerald, R. (2021). "Hidden in plain sight": expressing political criticism on Chinese social media. *Discourse Studies*, 23(3), 365–385. https://doi.org/10.1177/1461445620916365

Yang, G. (2018). Performing cyber-nationalism in twenty-first-century China: The case of Diba Expedition. In L. Hailong (Ed.), *From Cyber-Nationalism to Fandom Nationalism: The Case of Diba Expedition in China* (pp. 1-12). Routledge.

Yang, L. J., & Lim, K. C. (2010). *Three waves of nationalism in contemporary China: Sources, themes, presentations and consequences* (EAI Working Paper No. 155). ISSN 0219-1318, ISBN 978-981-08-6557-3.

Yuan, E. (2021). *The Web of meaning: the internet in a changing Chinese society*. Toronto: University of Toronto Press. https://doi.org/10.3138/9781487537623

Yue, Y. (2023, February 6). 粵語再次成爲熱搜 [Cantonese becomes trending topic again]. Wangyi. https://www.163.com/dy/article/HSTOGUL40537NJJQ.html

Zhang, C., & Ma, Y. (2023). Invented borders: the tension between grassroots patriotism and state-led patriotic campaigns in China. *Journal of Contemporary China*. DOI: 10.1080/10670564.2023.2167054

Zhang, X., & Guo, Z. (2012) Hegemony and counter-hegemony: the politics of dialects in TV programs in China. *Chinese Journal of Communication*, 5(3), 300-315, DOI: 10.1080/17544750.2012.701421

Zhang, Y., Liu, J., & Wen, J. (2018). Nationalism on Weibo: towards a multifaceted understanding of Chinese nationalism. *The China Quarterly*, 235, 758-783. doi:10.1017/S0305741018000863

Zhao, E. N., & Wu, Y. (2020, October 16). Over 80 percent of Chinese population speak Mandarin. *The People*. http://en.people.cn/n3/2020/1016/c90000-9769716.html

Zhao, L. M. (2019, April 19). 越來越多中國家庭正在放棄方言 [More and more Chinese family are giving up dialects]. *Huxiu*. https://www.huxiu.com/article/295231.html

Zhao, S. (2004). *A nation-state by construction: dynamics of modern Chinese nationalism*. Redwood City: Stanford University Press. https://doi.org/10.1515/9781503624498

Zhao, S. (2021) From affirmative to assertive patriots: nationalism in Xi Jinping's China. *The Washington Quarterly*, 44(4), 141-161. DOI: 10.1080/0163660X.2021.2018795

Zhao, X. J. (2018, March 8). 張歷君：語言與政治，從來連在一起 [Cheung Lik Kwan: language and politics always link together]. HK01. https://reurl.cc/ER0YX0

Zheng, Z. (2015, February 17). 中國最強方言是如何形成的 [How to form China's strongest dialect]. *The Paper*. https://www.thepaper.cn/newsDetail_forward_1298257

Zhong, Y., & Hwang, W. (2020). Why do Chinese democrats tend to be more nationalistic? Explaining popular nationalism in urban China. *Journal of Contemporary China*, 29(121), 61-74, DOI: 10.1080/10670564.2019.1621530

Zhou, B. (2015). Internet use, socio-geographic context, and citizenship engagement: A Multilevel Model on the Democratizing Effects of the Internet in China. In Yuan, Chen, W., and S. D. Reese (Eds.), (2015) *Networked China: global dynamics of digital media and civic engagement: new agendas in communication* (1st ed.). Routledge. https://doi.org/10.4324/9781315733074

Zhou, E. (1958, January 13). 當前文字改革的任務 [The current tasks of script reform]. http://www.gov.cn/gongbao/shuju/1958/gwyb195802.pdf

Zhou, M. (2011). Historical review of the PRC's minority/indigenous language policy and practice: nation-state building and identity construction. In G. H. Beckett, and G. A. Postiglione (Eds.), *China's Assimilationist Language Policy: The Impact on Indigenous/Minority Literacy and Social Harmony*. Routledge. https://doi.org/10.4324/9780203804070

Zhuang, M. (2016). Dialect program and the local media politics of Mainland China in the new era: the case of "Baixiao Talking Show". *Communication & Society*, 37, 161-189. DOI:10.30180/CS.201607_ (37).0007

Zhuang, Y., Huang, S., & Chen, C. (2022). Idolizing the nation: Chinese fandom nationalism through the Fangirl Expedition. *Chinese Journal of Communication*, 16(1), 53-72. DOI: 10.1080/17544750.2022.2108861

Appendix

The interview guide for the TV director Huang Jingyu

1. What caused you to make "Language Hero"?
2. Why the show ended at the fourth season in 2017?
3. Can you introduce the current Cantonese's situation in Guangzhou?
4. How did you select the team and individual participants to join the show?
5. Did you have an item bank to test participants?
6. I notice the design and sections of each season are different. How did you design and change those sections?
7. Why was the Cantonese section added to the fourth season while the previous three seasons did not have such change?
8. Did you receive any interruptions when you made and broadcasted the show?
9. Did you also run the show on Biknight Bili, Facebook, YouTube aside from WeChat and radio?
10. Can you provide the data of the viewing rate and audience's feedback?

The interview guide for the producer Buk Zai

1. Can you introduce your job?
2. How many people are in the team now?
3. What made you create the online Cantonese show? When did you start to realize the younger generation seldom speak Cantonese?
4. How do you design the theme of each episode? Where did you find the contents and materials of the show?
5. Can you introduce the business mode of the show?
6. What is the influence of the show currently? Can you provide the data to show the Cantonese and non-Cantonese audience's reaction and reflection?
7. Are you running Facebook and YouTube platforms for the show?

8. During the show creation and when it is being broadcasted, have you received any censorship?
9. What is your plan of the show?
10. What is your expectation to Cantonese's future?

The interview guide for the activist Lao Zhenyu

1. When did you find the young generation of Guangzhou start to do not speak Cantonese?
2. According to your observation, can you introduce current Cantonese's situation in Guangzhou? For example, do the Cantonese channels and programs increase or decrease?
3. What are the immigrant workers and the new Cantonese people's attitudes to Cantonese in the Pearl River Delta area?
4. Can you introduce or list the rules or laws to Cantonese from the government after the Shoring up movement in 2010?
5. As far as I know, the habitants of Guangzhou are making efforts to protect and promote Cantonese, such as the Speaking Cantonese Day and the first Cantonese textbook. What are the effects? Did you find other actions?
6. What do you think of the future of Cantonese?

The interview guide for the administrator Tony Li

1. Why did you set up the discussion group?
2. Can you talk about the event of the first generation of the group?
3. Can you introduce the components of the group members? How many are from Guangdong province?
4. Did you make a statistic of the topics within the group?
5. Do you review the contents generated by members?
6. How do you review the entry applications of the group?
7. What goal do you want to reach with this group?
8. Did you get any harassment and reposts to the group?
9. Do the administrators of the group also generate contents? If so, what is it?

10. Did you receive any feedback or advice to the group?
11. What do you think of Cantonese's future?

The interview guide for the researcher Rao Yuansheng

1. Can you tell me about your research and work?
2. What is Cantonese's situation in Guangdong now? Have you observed the decline of the Cantonese language among the younger generation? If so, when did you notice it?
3. I know that Cantonese has nine tones and six tones, and there are different versions of its pinyin system, but does Cantonese have its own writing system? If I type online, is there an easier way to write?
4. How has the Cantonese language changed from 30 years ago? How do you feel about Cantonese absorbing the vocabulary and usage of Mandarin?
5. Can you review the current Cantonese channels and programs in Guangdong Province? Have there been any changes in them?
6. Have you paid attention to the creation of Cantonese in new media? For example, online radio, live or online stand-up comedy, and especially Cantonese programs on social media.
7. Do you have any concerns about initiatives organized by individuals or groups in the community to protect the Cantonese language? Can you tell us about and evaluate the effectiveness of these initiatives?
8. In your opinion, has the central government and the Guangdong Provincial Government protected, developed or suppressed the Cantonese language? Do you know about the "Chinese Language Protection Project"? How do you see the impact of the integration of the Greater Bay Area on the Cantonese language?
9. What do you think about the future of the Cantonese language?

Index

A
ATV, xxvii

B
Bao Dong Gua, 24

C
Canton Fair, xxvii
Chinese dream, xxxvi
consumer nationalism, xxxiv
culturalism, xxxi

D
Diba Expedition, xxxv

F
Fangirl Expedition, xxxv
Fen Qing, xxxiv
filial nationalism, xxxiv

G
Greater Bay Area, 7
Guangzhou, xxiii, xxv, xxvii, xxviii, xxix, xli, xliii, 5, 7, 9, 10, 11, 16, 19, 21, 31, 32, 34, 36, 37, 43, 44, 51, 52, 55, 57, 58, 62, 63, 67, 68, 69, 72, 73, 74, 75, 79, 80
Guanhua, 1
Gwong Dung Jan, 66
Gwong Zau Jan, 62
Gwong Zau Waa, 9

H
Hanyu Shuiping Kaoshi, 6

J
Ji Jing Bou Jing, 37
Ji Tau, 36
Jyutping, 57

K
Kung Hei Fat Choy, 19

L
Laau, 54
Leng Zai, 37
Lingnan, 1
little pinks, xxxv
Long Wun, 38

M
Mao era, xxvii, xxxii, xxxvii
Me Aa, 23
Migrant Wives, Local Husbands, 36

N
Naam Jyut empire, xxix
National Security Law, 64

P

parodic satire, xl
Putonghua Proficiency Test, 5

R

Ruguan Xue, xxxiv

S

Si Shu, 15

T

Tang people, 56
Television Southern, xxviii
The King of Naam Jyut, xxix

The Lanfang Republic, 46
the language of Guangdong, 9
TVB, xxvii

V

virtual private networks, xxxv

W

White Paper movement, xl
wolf warrior diplomacy, xxxvi

Y

Yayan, 1
Yue language, 1

www.ingramcontent.com/pod-product-compliance
Lightning Source LLC
Chambersburg PA
CBHW051103230426
43667CB00013B/2422